# CROSSING TO KILL

# CROSSING TO KILL

## The True Story of the Serial-Killer Playground

### Simon Whitechapel

This updated edition first published in 2002 by

Virgin Books Ltd
Thames Wharf Studios
Rainville Road
London W6 9HA

First edition published 2000

*www.virgin.com/books*

Typeset by TW Typesetting, Plymouth, Devon

Printed and bound by Mackays of Chatham PLC

ISBN 0 7535 0686 6

Parts of *Crossing to Kill* express political and social views that
some may find controversial or offensive. The author would like
to state clearly that they are his views alone and not those of
Virgin Books or its employees.

# CONTENTS

A todos los sufrientes de Ciudad Juárez

'Power is poison.' [Alan Moore. Interview in *The Edge* (see http.//www.users.globalnet.co.uk/~houghtong/edge.htm)]

'Even the devil is afraid of living here.' [Remark of Juárez inhabitant reported in Charles Bowden's 'While You Were Sleeping' (*Harper's* magazine, December 1996)]

'Tonight, John Quinones takes you into their world, where young women desperate for jobs are being stalked by a nameless, faceless predator . . . You're in the Mexican desert, just a stone's throw from the American border, on the trail of mass murder.' ('Silent Screams in Juarez', ABC's *20–20* current affairs programme, Wednesday, 20 January 1999)

'*Te Mereces La Silla Eléctrica*' ('You Deserve the Electric Chair'). [Headline from *El Diario de Juárez* (*The Juárez Daily*), reporting the words of a young woman sexually assaulted by Jesús Manuel Guardado Márquez, alias '*El Dracula*']

'e$^{i\pi}$EB1.' [Leonhard Euler (1707–1803)]

'Regenbogen am Morgen macht dem Schäfer Sorgen; Regenbogen am Abend ist dem Schäfer Labend.' [Friedrich Wilhelm Nietzsche (1844–1900)]

'ἐὰν δὲ ἐκπιέξῃς μυκτῆρας ἐκελεύσεται αἷμα.' [*The Septuagint* (c. 100 BC)]

## ACKNOWLEDGEMENTS

First, I would like to thank Héctor Carreon of the ParaSagrario Consortium for his response to enquiries made by the author and publisher. The Consortium was created in memory of María Sagrario González Flores, a seventeen-year-old girl who was one of the victims of the serial killings in Juárez, and its website can be found at http://www.aztlan.net/ParaSagrario.[1]

However, I wish to stress that neither Mr Carreon nor any other member of the Consortium has seen or approved any part of *Crossing to Kill* before publication, and its contents remain the sole responsibility of the author.

I'd also like to thank Charles Bowden for his help with contacts and for his article on Juárez, 'While You Were Sleeping' (*Harper's* magazine, 1996), which was an invaluable reference and was incorporated into his book *Juárez: The Laboratory of our Future* (Aperture, 1998); the photographers Jaime Bailléres and Julián Cardona of Ciudad Juárez;[2] the other journalists in México, the United States, and elsewhere who have written about the serial killings, in particular Tim Madigan for his detailed series of articles; and all members of the Internet community who provided assistance with material, in particular members of the sci.lang.translation newsgroup and Jason Pope and Joe of alt.true-crime.[3] Again, I wish to stress that no one outside Virgin Publishing who helped with the book had any advance notice of its contents, which remain the sole responsibility of the author.

---

[1] Affiliated to the ParaSagrario Consortium is Casa Amiga, a group working for women's rights in Ciudad Juárez. Donations can be sent to the following address: Casa Amiga, Centro De Crisis, Peru Norte 878, Col. Hidalgo, Cd. Juárez, Chihuahua, C.P. 32312, México.
[2] Señores Bailléres's and Cardona's agent can be contacted at jazzblues@aol.com
[3] For further details of Joe's true-crime mailing list and Jason's serial killer website, please visit http://members.aol.com/Joe1orbit/MailingList1.html and http://www.btinternet.com/~serial.killer/

Further thanks go to David M. Mitchell of Oneiros Books,[4] James Williamson of Creation Books, and the former *Headpress* editor David Slater for affording me many valuable insights into aspects of the psychopathic personality; to James Williamson again for supplying a Spanish/English dictionary that has proved very useful during the writing of this book; to the current *Headpress* editor David Kerekes for permission to quote from the Critical Vision compilation *Critical Vision* (1995) and Jesús Ignacio Aldapuerta's short-story collection *The Eyes* (1995); to Rodolfo Compte of Buenos Aires for help with the Spanish; to Richard Wagner, Photographed by Lightning, Psycho-Testudo, and Heydrich for musical accompaniment; finally and particularly, my thanks go to James Marriott of Virgin Books, without whom this book could never have appeared.

Simon Whitechapel, London, 1999

Note: In Mexican Spanish (Ciudad) Juárez is pronounced something like (see-oo-DAAD) HWAA-ress, with the 'h' pronounced like the 'ch' of the Scottish 'loch', German 'Buch', or Yiddish 'chutzpah'.

---

[4]For further details of Oneiros Books, please visit http://www.freeyellow. com/members6/oneiros/index.html

# Chronology

*Cronología f. Ciencia que tiene por objeto determinar el orden y las fechas de los acontecimientos históricos.*

Chronology: A science that attempts to determine the order and dates of historical events.

c. 1947. Birth of Abdul Latif Sharif Sharif (sic) in Egypt. Five decades later, at a deportation hearing in the United States, he will testify to a troubled childhood, claiming that he suffered repeated sexual abuse from his father and other male relatives.

1970. Sharif emigrates to the United States, living at first in New York. He begins to establish a reputation for drunkenness and promiscuity that will accompany him for the remainder of his stay in the United States.

1971. Birth of Victor Moreno Rivera, who will later be charged as an accomplice of Sharif.

1973. Birth of Jesús Manuel Guardado Márquez, also later to be charged as an accomplice of Sharif.

3 January 1977. A missing airline hostess called Sandra Miller is found by police just as she dies from a single stab-wound on a roadside in Pennsylvania. Blood and clumps of hair are found in the snow near her home at Flemington, New Jersey, leading the police to conclude that she was violently abducted and driven across the Delaware River to the scene of her death. The police are unable to find the killer, but two decades later, as news of Sharif's crimes reaches them from México, tell the media that he is now the prime suspect. Sharif was working for Magnesium Electron of New Jersey at the time, and is known to have frequented the same bars as Sandra Miller.

1978. Sharif has been fired from another job in New Jersey for suspected expense account fraud and has moved to New Hope, Pennsylvania. An acquaintance called John Pascoe will later recall his interest in and ability to attract young girls, including, Pascoe claims, under-age ones. The girls often mysteriously disappear from the area having last been seen in Sharif's apartment. Pascoe grows disturbed about Sharif's behaviour, later recalling, among other incidents, a deer-hunting expedition in local woods during which Sharif tortures a wounded buck.

1980. Pascoe and Sharif fall out when Pascoe enters his apartment without permission and finds the meagre possessions of Sharif's latest conquest – 'petite, pretty, with long, light-blonde hair' – still there, despite Sharif's assertion that she had left for good. Sharif orders Pascoe out of the apartment, and as he leaves he sees a mud-caked shovel in Sharif's front porch.

1981. Sharif has moved to Palm Beach, Florida, to work for a company called Cercoa Inc. On 2 May, he rapes a twenty-three-year-old woman called Tracey. Cercoa Inc., which has created a department specially for him, finds the best legal defence team for their wayward but brilliant employee, but on August 13th, on the eve of the trial, he rapes and assaults another woman called Ruth in West Palm Beach. The police there do not pass details of the second rape to their colleagues, and Sharif gains probation for his attack on Tracey and serves only 45 days for his attack on Ruth.

1982. Fired by Cercoa Inc. because of his legal difficulties, Sharif moves to Gainesville, Florida.

1983. A short-lived marriage ends when Sharif beats his wife unconscious, and he places an ad in the *Gainesville Sun* for a live-in housekeeper. A twenty-year-old college student called Lisa answers the ad and moves in on 17 March. Sharif repeatedly rapes and beats her the same night, threatening to kill her: 'I will bury you out back in the woods. I've done it before, and I'll do it again.' He is arrested and imprisoned to await trial.

January 1984. While awaiting trial, Sharif escapes from Alachua County Jail with a group of other prisoners. He is soon recaptured.

31 January 1984. Sharif is sentenced to twelve years for the rape of Lisa. The assistant State Attorney Gordon Groland promises Lisa that on his release he will be 'met at the prison gates and escorted to the plane' for deportation back to Egypt.

October 1989. Sharif is released after serving less than half of his sentence. No state officials are waiting at the prison gates. A fortnight later he is working for Benchmark Research and Technology, an oil company in Midland, Texas. He soon re-establishes a reputation for drunkenness and promiscuity, but simultaneously confirms his reputation as a 'brilliant chemist', helping Benchmark punch well above its weight in the oil business. The United States Department of Energy marks him out for attention and he is photographed shaking hands in his laboratory with the US senator Phil Gramm.

1991. Sharif is arrested for drunk-driving for the second time in Midland and starts attending meetings of Alcoholics Anonymous. Tom Wilson, a colleague from his Florida days, is now working with him at Benchmark and, aware that he should have been deported after the rape of Lisa in Florida, reports him to the US Border Patrol.

1992. Sharif is arrested and a deportation hearing gets under way in El Paso, Texas, separated by the width of the Rio Grande from Ciudad Juárez, México, which has become famous for its foreign-owned *maquiladora* factories employing thousands of young women. At the hearing United States Immigration Judge William Nail hears testimony in favour of Sharif from colleagues at Benchmark and members of his Alcoholics Anonymous group.

28 September 1993. Judge Nail acknowledges the positive testimony but decides against Sharif, citing his recent arrests for drunk-driving as evidence of his continuing tendency to abuse alcohol and undergo 'a remarkable transformation . . . much like the principal character in Robert Louis Stevenson's popular story, *The Strange Case of Dr Jekyll and Mr Hyde*.' Sharif's lawyers immediately appeal against the deportation order and Sharif is freed on bail to await the second hearing, also in El Paso. It is during this period that he is believed to have first begun to travel regularly to Juárez for visits to the sleazy nightclub district of Ugarte.

31 October (Hallowe'en) 1993. Sharif meets a woman called Ann at a nightclub in Midland and takes her back to the home he still owns there. He attacks her and rapes her repeatedly till dawn. Faced with a second serious charge

against his client, Jack Ladd, Sharif's chief lawyer in the deportation hearings, proposes a deal to the American authorities: if the charges are dismissed, Sharif will leave the United States for good.

May 1994. Before the authorities have responded to the proposal, Sharif acts on his own initiative and emigrates to Juárez to work for Benchmark in one of the *maquiladora* factories.

August 1994. The authorities accept Ladd's proposal and the charges against Sharif are dismissed. Wayne Kinsey, the Benchmark CEO (Chief Executive Officer), later claims that Sharif stopped working for Benchmark a few months after his arrival in México. The corpses of raped and murdered young women have started to turn up in the suburbs of Juárez and the surrounding desert, casting a spell of fear over the city. Many of the victims have last been seen in Ugarte, where Sharif is now a familiar figure, freely spending the money he earns from another well-paid job as he flirts and dances with young women from the *maquiladoras*.

Summer 1995. Sharif is seen frequently in the company of a seventeen-year-old *maquiladora* worker called Elizabeth Castro García, a 'slender, beautiful girl with long, dark hair'.

15 August 1995. Elizabeth Castro García disappears. Her strangled body turns up four days later beside a highway in southern Juárez.

Early October 1995. A young woman called Blanca accuses Sharif of subjecting her to three days of rape and beatings at his home in Rincones de San Marcos, an exclusive district in north-western Juárez. She tells the police that he also threatened to murder her and dump her body in Lote Bravo, a patch of desert to the south of the city where many of the previous murder victims have been found. A few days later she withdraws the charges and disappears, but the Mexican police have now begun to investigate Sharif's links with the rapes and murders of *maquiladora* workers, and learn of his criminal record in the United States. Sharif is charged with the murder of Elizabeth Castro García and held in the Juárez *Centro de Readaptación Social para Adultos*, or the Centre for the Social Rehabilitation of Adults, known for short as the

*CeReSo*, where he awaits trial in the notoriously slow Mexican legal system. Following his arrest the rapes and murders have stopped but Sharif continues to insist that he is innocent.

1995–1996. It is later alleged by the Juárez police that during this period Sharif receives regular visits in the *CeReSo* from members of a Juárez street-gang called *Los Rebeldes*, The Rebels, who are led by Sergio Armendáriz, nicknamed *El Diablo*, The Devil.

1996. Sharif is still firmly behind bars but the rapes and murders of young women have started again, throwing the inhabitants of Juárez into a renewed frenzy of fear, mingled this time with anger at the seeming inability of the authorities to solve the crimes.

April, 1996. After tip-offs from the criminal underworld in Ugarte, the police arrest Sergio Armendáriz and the other members of *Los Rebeldes*, accusing them of a conspiracy with Sharif. They allege Sharif has been paying them to rape and murder in an attempt to establish his innocence of the previous crimes. *Los Rebeldes* insist they are innocent of the charge, accusing the police of torturing them into false confessions. Following their arrest, the rapes and murders stop for the second time.

1996–present. Members of *Los Rebeldes* fight legal battles with the authorities over their arrest. Some are released, none have yet been put on trial for the crimes of which they are accused, although the authorities are confident they have sufficient evidence to secure convictions, including bite-marks on the bodies of some of the victims that match the teeth of *El Diablo*.

Autumn, 1997. Victor Moreno Rivera, an American citizen living in El Paso, Texas, and with convictions for drug trafficking, visits the Juárez *CeReSo* to see a friend being held there. He also, the police later allege, meets Sharif for the first time and establishes a friendship with him.

Early 1998. The bodies of raped and murdered young women start appearing again in the desert around Juárez. The city is gripped by renewed terror and the hunt for the criminals becomes increasingly politicised.

18 February 1999. A fifteen-year-old girl later identified only as Susana is raped and assaulted by a man called Jesús

Manuel Guardado Márquez, alias *El Dracula* or *El Tolteca*. Too frightened to report the attack to the police at the time, she will later come forward when Márquez appears in the media accused of a similar attack on another young girl.

3 March 1999. Sharif is finally put on trial for the murder of Elizabeth Castro García, is found guilty, and is sentenced to thirty years' imprisonment. This is the maximum possible sentence for murder under Mexican law, which does not possess the death penalty.

18 March 1999. A fourteen-year-old girl later identified only as Nancy stumbles bleeding and weeping into a stranger's home in the desert around southern Juárez. She is taken to the police and tells them that she has been raped and half-strangled by the driver of one of the *maquiladora* buses. He had abducted her when she became the final passenger on the bus taking her home from the *maquiladora* where she has been working for the past three weeks, after passing herself off as a seventeen-year-old with borrowed identification. The bus driver is identified as Jesús Manuel Guardado Márquez, alias *El Dracula* or *El Tolteca*. Unaware as yet of his attack on Susana, the police nevertheless discover he has a previous conviction for sexual assault, but when they set out to arrest him he has already fled from Juárez with his pregnant wife.

March 1999. In hiding in a town called Gómez Palacio, Durango state, a few hundred kilometres south of Juárez, *El Tolteca* attacks his wife and is reported by his sister to the police, who arrest him and, Márquez later alleges, assault him. He is returned to Juárez, where he later alleges he is assaulted by police again. He makes a confession implicating four other men in the rape and murder of *maquiladora* workers: Augustín Toribio Castillo, *El Kiani*, José Gaspar Ceballos Chavez, *El Gaspy*, Victor Moreno Rivera, *El Narco*, and Bernardo Hernando Fernández, *El Samber*. The five men, all of whom worked as bus drivers for the *maquiladora* companies, are nicknamed *Los Choferes*, The Drivers, by the media, and the police claim they have all confessed to being part of another paid conspiracy organised by Sharif from behind bars. Using Moreno as his contact, Sharif has been paying them to rape and murder two young women a month in another attempt to establish his innocence of the first series of crimes. While not maintaining his innocence, Márquez accuses the police of assault; the other four now maintain their innocence and accuse the police of torturing false confessions out of them. Susana has now come forward to report Márquez's rape of her in February. Following the arrest of Los Choferes, the rapes and murders in Juárez have stopped for the third time.

March 1999. A scandal erupts in the Juárez media when, as part of the investigations into the alleged conspiracy between Sharif and Los Choferes, it is discovered that Sharif is enjoying extraordinary privileges in the Juárez CeReSo, including use of a cell-phone on which he has been making regular unsupervised calls to the outside world in pursuit of his claims of innocence. Links are established between Sharif and an American currency-forger called Newton van Drunen, whom he had befriended in the CeReSo and who is now serving a sentence in Chicago. Police allege that van Drunen has been sending money to Sharif with which he paid Los Choferes to take part in the conspiracy of rape and murder.

April 1999. Seemingly as a direct result of media pressure, the director of the CeReSo in Juárez is dismissed and Sharif is moved from Juárez to a maximum security cell in Chihuahua, the capital of Chihuahua state, where, at the time of writing, he remains.

1999–present. The legal and political echoes of this extraordinary series of rapes and murders, charges and counter-charges, continue to reverberate through México and the United States, and include persistent allegations that Sharif had influential friends in Mexican politics and the Mexican judiciary.

## UPDATE

In the first edition of Crossing to Kill I wrote that 'the legal and political echoes of this extraordinary series of rapes and murders, charges and counter-charges, continue to reverberate through Mexico and the United States'. Two years on, the echoes are as loud as ever and the question now seems less that of *when* they will die than that of *whether* they will die.

Sharif was suspected of many murders but convicted of only one. That conviction has now been overturned. The murders seemed to stop with his arrest . . . then began again . . . then seemed to stop with the arrest of his alleged accomplices, members of a gang called The Rebels . . . then began again . . . then seemed to stop again with the arrest of *more* of his alleged accomplices – members of a group of bus drivers headed by a man nicknamed *El Dracula*.

And now the murders have started again.

The latest victim, seventeen-year-old Lilia Alejandra García Andrade, was discovered raped and murdered on 21 Feb 2001 in an empty lot situated in a well-traversed section of the city. García, a single mother of two young children, was last reported seen leaving work in the afternoon one week earlier on St Valentine's Day. Similar to many other victims, she worked in a maquiladora export plant.[1]

What is going on? I asked that question two years ago and I am asking it now. One of the very few certainties in the case was that almost nothing is certain. That remains true. Groping blindfolded in a morass of speculation and counter-speculation, one can close one's hand only rarely over a nugget of hard, objectively verifiable fact.

31 March 2000. Almost a year to the day after he was sentenced to thirty years for the murder of Elizabeth Castro García, Sharif succeeds in having the conviction overturned on grounds that insufficient evidence was presented by the prosecution. The authorities of the state of Chihuahua immediately brought fresh charges against him and he remains as of this writing in a high-security cell in the state capital, Chihuahua City. One step forward, one step back.

1999–2001. Further members of *Los Rebeldes* are released for lack of evidence, among them one José Luis Rosales, and the authorities' allegations of a conspiracy between Sharif and the gang as a whole look increasingly difficult to substantiate. However, forensic evidence uncovered after the release of Rosales implicates him again in the crimes and the authorities appeal against the original release. It is overturned and a

---

[1] http://www.us-mex.org/borderlines/updater/2001/mar8terror.html#reign

warrant is issued for his re-arrest. Months pass and the warrant remains unfulfilled while Rosales remains in hiding, probably across the border in the United States.

23 February 2001. Rosales is arrested in Dallas, Texas, a few hundred kilometres from the scene of his alleged crimes in Ciudad Juárez. A day later, as American police try to determine whether he can be linked to any similar crimes in Dalls, he is deported to Mexico. His family maintain his innocence and say that the Medican authorities have made a serious mistake.

It's not an implausible claim. Whatever else the authorities may have managed to achieve in Juárez, putting a stop to the sex killings is not one of the them. The fact that Sharif's arrest did not stop them, nor the arrest of *Los Rebeldes*, nor the arrest of *Los Choferes*, proves one thing: if Sharif and his alleged accomplices are sex killers, they are not the only ones in Juárez. Another suspect appeared after a woman alleged that she had been imprisoned for eight months by a man who kept her shaven-headed and chained and tortured her by burning her breasts and vagina with cigarettes. The story appeared in the media under the headline, 'Chained and Horribly Abused for Eight Months'. Indeed, when she did escape, in the two days that it took her to reach Casa Amiga (after being taken in and helped by a local family) the perpetrator had persuaded the police by means of her 'therapy' records that she had a history of mental instability, and that charges brought against him were false.[2]

In a city of 1,000,000 people – or is it 2,000,000? – there are bound to be psychopaths, and if the Juárez police are as inept and dilatory as relatives of the serial-murder victims have persistently alleged, some of those psychopaths are almost bound to be getting away with murder. Literally.

---

[2]http://www/nmsu.edu/~frontera/oct00/feat2.html

# 1. Slaughter

*Matanza f. (1) Acción de matar a una o varias personas. (2) Exterminio, hecatombe.*

Slaughter: (1) The action of killing one or more persons. (2) Extermination, great sacrifice.

Count to ten. Say each number slowly, carefully: one, two, three, four, five, six, seven, eight, nine, ten. Then do it again, in Spanish: uno, dos, tres, cuatro, cinco, seis, siete, ocho, nueve, diez.

And again, in Nahuatl:[1] cě, ŏme, ěyi, nǎhui, mǎcuïlli, chicuacě, chicŏme, chicuěyi, chiucnǎhui, ma'tlactli.

Then do all of that – English, Spanish, Nahuatl – five more times.

And each number of the one hundred and eighty will be a destroyed life. The life of a young woman in the Mexican border city of Juárez during the final decade of the twentieth century. A young woman murdered. Often raped. Sometimes tortured or mutilated. Dumped in the nearby desert, or a gutter or alleyway in the city itself. Dozens more young women are missing, presumed raped and murdered in the same way and by the same men.

## asesinar v. t. Matar alevosamente

The Spanish word for murder is *asesino*, related to the English 'assassin'. Related too, some say, to the Arabic *hašiiš* – hashish. The story goes that a fanatical Islamic sect of medieval Syria used the drug to reward and enslave its adherents, sending them forth from its remote mountain fastness to slay, eager to earn the right to return and suck the heavy scent of *hašiiš* into their lungs again.

The inhabitants of Juárez know heavy scents too. The metallic tangs and stinks of industrial pollution from the

---

[1] The main Amerindian language spoken in present-day México.

foreign-owned *maquiladora* factories. Flavoured dusts and grits borne in on the wind from the rubbish-strewn suburbs and the outlying desert. Rotting food and animal carcasses in the city's dumps. The algal reek of the polluted *Río Bravo* – 'The Rio Grande' in English. And, sometimes, cheap perfume mingled with sweat and blood and semen. The heavy scents of a young woman's corpse lying in a gutter or alleyway.

## Blood

*Sangre f. Líquido rojo que circula por las venas y las arterias de los vertebrados.*
Blood: A red liquid that circulates through the veins and arteries of vertebrates.

'*Festinant ut effundant sanguinem innocentem.*' ('They make haste to shed innocent blood.') (Isaiah, lix, 7)

## Why?

In Spanish there are two ways of saying it: '*¿Por qué?*' and '*¿Para qué?*'. '*¿Por qué?*' means 'What causes?'. '*¿Para qué?*' means 'What intentions?'.

*Crossing to Kill* will try to answer both questions. Why have more than one hundred and eighty young Mexican women been raped and murdered over the past decade? Why are dozens more missing? Why has this taken place in one city on the Mexican–American border?

*¿Por qué?* Imagine a young woman writhing on desert sand with a trident buried in her guts. One prong is Mexican history. One is Mexican Catholicism. One is Mexican politics.

## History

*Historia f. (1) Desarrollo de la vida de la humanidad. (2) Narración verdadera y ordenada de los acontecimientos pasados y las cosas memorables de la actividad humana.*
History: (1) Unfolding of the life of humanity. (2) Faithful and ordered narration of past events and memorable happenings in human activity.

México is an ancient land. Its very name comes from an alternative term for the Aztecs in Nahuatl, and its present-day boundaries enclose the territories of all the familiar kingdoms and empires of pre-Columbian history: the Aztecs, the Mayas, the Olmecs, the Toltecs; and most of the unfamiliar ones: the Zapotecs, the Totonacs, the Teotihuacans, the Mixtecs. It is impossible to find definite divisions between these peoples and their languages and cultures: borrowings and mutual influences were innumerable and frequent – particularly in religion. Gods like Quetzalcoatl, Huitzilopochtli, and Tezcatlipoca were known all over the region under varying names, all of them tongue-twisting, no doubt, in a Western mouth. The meanings of these names are no less mind-twisting in a Western head: 'The Feathered Serpent', 'The Lefthand Hummingbird', 'The Smoking Mirror'.

Such surrealism and psychedelia are familiar in Western art and popular music, and may have had the same origin in pre-Columbian Meso-America: the use of mind-altering chemicals. Another shared element of Meso-American religion was (and is) the ritual consumption of psychoactive fungi and herbs, often by the inhalation of their fumes or smoke. Modern botany commemorates the practice in the scientific names bestowed on some of them: amongst the members of the famously (and infamously) psychoactive mushroom genus *Psilocybe* are *Psilocybe mexicana* – Mexican psilocybe, and *Psilocybe aztecorum* – Psilocybe of the Aztecs (*The Encyclopedia of Psychoactive Drugs: Mushrooms: Psychoactive Fungi*, Peter E. Furst, Burke Publishing, 1988). But the most famous shared element of Meso-American religion was, of course, human sacrifice:

During the second ritual month of the Aztec year, *Tlacaxipehualiztli* – 'Flaying of Men' – the priests killed human victims by removing their hearts. They flayed the bodies and put on the skins, which were dyed yellow and called *teocuitlaquemitl* – 'golden clothes'. Other victims were fastened to a frame and put to death with arrows. Their blood dripping down was believed to symbolise the fertile spring rains. (*Encyclopedia Britannica*, entry for '*Xipe Totec*' – Nahuatl for 'Our Lord the Flayed One', under 'Aztec Religion'.)

Such deities and their thirst for blood were not forgotten after the Spanish conquest. On the contrary, some were incorporated into the saintly hierarchies of the new religion imposed on the conquered peoples, and the Mayan rain and compass god Chac, for example, lent attributes to Christian saints and took up the Spanish-imported innovation of horse-riding. Another Spanish-imported innovation was an expansion of the ideology and iconography of human sacrifice. Pre-Columbian religion overwhelmingly concentrated on the death and torture of men. The Spanish conquest would change all that.

## Religion

*Religión f. Conjunto de creencias o dogmas acerca de la divinidad: religión cristiana.*

Religion. Collection of beliefs or dogmas related to God or gods: *the Christian religion.*

The *conquistadores* brought another death cult to México. It was called the Roman Catholic Church. Her greatest antagonist, Protestantism, was being born at exactly the same time as the Aztec empire was dying – Luther was excommunicated and his beliefs outlawed in 1521, halfway through the Spanish conquest of México – and she was fighting back on battlefields both of the sword and of the mind. She consciously increased the splendour and appeal of her rituals and architecture, and the new art and sculpture she commissioned began to re-emphasise one of the most ancient and powerful of all psychological archetypes – the violent and painful death of beautiful young women:

St Agatha; represented in Christian art with a pair of shears, and holding in her hand a salver, on which her breasts are placed. The reference is to her martyrdom, when her breasts were cut off by a pair of shears.

St Catharine; a virgin of royal descent in Alexandria, who publicly confessed the Christian faith at a sacrificial feast held by the Emperor Maximinus, for which confession she was put to death by torture by means of a wheel like that of a chaff-cutter.

St Lucy; it is said that a nobleman wanted to marry her for the beauty of her eyes; so she tore them out and gave them to him saying, 'Now let me live to God'. The story says that her eyesight was restored; but her rejected lover accused her of faith in Christ, and she was martyred by a sword thrust into her neck. (All short hagiographies adapted from *Brewer's Dictionary of Phrase and Fable*, E. Cobham Brewer, 1894.)

In Catholic art these virgin-martyrs are represented at the height of their beauty and sexual attractiveness: as slender, long-haired teenaged girls. Like the victims of Juárez:

> *Todas las mujeres eran muy jóvenes, esbeltas, de larga y oscura cabellera.* All the women were very young, slender, with long, dark hair. ('*En Ciudad Juárez Capturaron a los Asesinos de 17 Jóvenes Mujeres*' – 'The Murderers of 17 Young Women are arrested in Juárez', Adriana Candia, *El Diario De Juárez*)

The power of both sets of deaths derives, I believe, from the waste it represents: fertile young women are wantonly sacrificed to nourish, on the one hand, the patriarchal religion of a male trinity, and, on the other, the pleasure of a serial-killer, or serial-killers. *Sanguis martyrum semen ecclesiæ*: the blood of martyrs is the seed of the church. And the female workers of Juárez may have had to bleed for the masters of the *maquiladoras*, the foreign-owned factories, in order to bleed for the master, or masters, of the desert. They may have had to prove that they were not pregnant; that they were still fertile:

> Workers at one plant complain of a company rule requiring new female hires to present bloody tampons for three consecutive months. (Charles Bowden, 'While You Were Sleeping'.)

But even more prominent amongst the female archetypes of Catholicism than the bleeding virgin-martyrs is, of course, another young woman. Alongside the saints Lucy and Agatha and Catherine, roasted or pierced, beheaded or sliced, is the *Beata Virgen María*, the Blessed Virgin Mary, very often represented as a slender, long-haired teenaged girl presenting her left nipple to the lips of the infant Messiah:

In what may be a 'signature' of the killer, the shoes of at least one of the recent victims were placed neatly beside her body, similar to that of four victims last year. Also, the left breast of at least one was mutilated, similar to some of the earlier cases. (SIX NEW SLAYINGS REVEAL THAT KILLER STILL ON THE LOOSE, Mark Smith, *Houston Chronicle*, 30 March 1996)

In Christian doctrine the *Virgo Maria*, the Virgin Mary, later becomes the *Mater Dolorosa*, the Agonised Mother, mind racked and twisted by grief as she weeps over the bruised and blood-encrusted corpse of her grown-up child.

This beauty of female pain and suffering in God's sight has been a constant theme of Catholic teaching, harmonising smoothly with another theme: the beauty of poverty and hard work for one's divinely appointed masters. So well was this doctrine enforced on the native inhabitants of México that the Spanish word *peón*, meaning 'peasant', was taken into English first for an enforced labourer in the southern states of America and then as a generic term for 'any very poor person'. These twin Christian virtues of suffering and poverty also fit very well today with the intentions of México's secular businessmen and politicians and their counterparts in the United States.

## Politics

*Maquiladora f. Méx. Planta que ejecuta, para una empresa más importante, una de las operaciones del proceso de fabricación de un producto.*

Maquiladora. (Mexican Spanish.) A factory that carries out one of the operations in the manufacture of a product for a larger company.

In Spanish a *maquiladora*, with one 'l', is a Mexican factory producing goods for an overseas firm; a *maquilladora*, with two 'l's, is a woman who applies make-up to herself. The two lie side by side in a Spanish dictionary, and come together in reality every working day in Juárez, most obviously when the white buses provided by foreign firms begin to drop off their passengers after work:

Hundreds of those who descend are waiflike teenage girls, wearing bright red lipstick and *maquiladora* smocks. They have come in the past few months from farms and villages in every state in Mexico, some from as far away as Oaxaca or Chiapas in the far south. (WHO IS KILLING THE WOMEN OF JUAREZ?, Tim Madigan, *Fort Worth Star-Telegram*, 16 March 1999)

In 1980, the population of Juárez was 567,000; in 1999, it is estimated at two million, and rising fast. Such growth in an organ of the human body would be regarded as cancerous, and cancerous Juárez certainly is, in another sense:

There's a whole *maquiladora* corridor along the border, with incredible levels of lead in the water, high levels of pollution and toxic waste, and workers working for five dollars a day. (David Barsamian, *Keeping the Rabble in Line: Interviews with Noam Chomsky*, p. 43, words of David Barsamian)

Juárez is perhaps the paradigm of a Mexican border city, separated by the width of the Río Bravo and a heavily guarded bridge and security fences from El Paso, Texas (population 425,000 in 1980; 583,000 in 1999). Juárez is so near to the fabled luxury and wealth of North America – and yet so far. American laws end at the border, and that is why American companies have been pouring across it, eager to take advantage of cheap Mexican labour and lax Mexican laws on pollution and industrial relations. Construction of *maquiladoras* in Juárez has matched the growth in population: there are now said to be three hundred in the city.

*Maquiladoras* need *obreras* – workers, particularly women. Young women, with nimble fingers, undimmed eyes, and empty purses. For these are the ones who will be prepared to put up with the long hours and harsh conditions of employment. Who will regard the chance to shower at work as a luxury. Who will travel thousands of kilometres and live in slums reeking with sewage for the *chance* of work, let alone its reality. *A quien dan, no escoge.* Beggars cannot be choosers.

And beggars cannot, in México, be other than Amerindian or *mestizo*, that is, of mixed Amerindian and European stock. It could hardly be otherwise, for the overwhelming majority of the population are of this origin – perhaps ninety-seven per cent, according to one estimate (*Encyclopedia Britannica*, entry for 'Mexico').

So it is that the female workers of the *maquiladoras* of Juárez are Amerindian or *mestiza*, and so it is that the rapes and murders of some of them begin to resonate powerfully with a long-standing erotic tradition of Western popular culture: the dark-haired Amerindian beauty in a world of violence and upheaval.

Disney's 1995 movie *Pocahontas* demonstrates the power of the tradition but offers a prettified and saccharine version of it. A much harsher, and specifically Mexican, version demonstrates also the age of the tradition: H. Rider Haggard's *Montezuma's Daughter* (1892) contains a description of a beautiful Mexican princess being stripped naked and strapped to a sacrificial altar with the white man she loves:

> Turning to Otomie I began to bid her farewell in a clear voice, when to my amazement I saw that as I had been served so she was being served, for her splendid robes were torn off her and she stood before me arrayed in nothing but her beauty, her flowing hair, and a broidered cotton smock.
>
> 'Do not wonder, Teule [white man],' she said in a low voice, answering the question my tongue refused to frame, 'I am your wife and yonder [on the altar of sacrifice] is our marriage bed, the first and last. Though you do not love me, today I die your death and at your side, as I have the right to do. I could not save you, Teule, but at least I can die with you.' (Chapter xxi)

But Rider Haggard's book stands at the beginning of the tradition, which would flourish more rankly in the following century, bearing such mottled, strongly flavoured fruit as:

> She went for him with her hands and mouth right away. She cupped his heavy sack in her hands and slid his hard

manhood into her mouth slowly, eyes open and watching it disappear inch by inch. When she had as much in her mouth as she could take, she closed her eyes and slid one hand to the base of his shaft, holding it there while she sucked on it eagerly.

He doubted she had learned this in an Indian camp, and surmised that she had been with a few white men before in her twenty-odd years.

'She' being – with long hair 'black as a raven's wing' – the Amerindian girl Katy Little Flower of J.R. Roberts' *The Bounty Women* (1984), the thirty-fifth book in the porn-western *Gunsmith* series. But even as it bore such mottled fruit, the tradition was setting gnarled underground tubers, one of which is unearthed by the American feminist Andrea Dworkin in her book *Letters from a Warzone*, where she describes a clandestinely distributed 1980s computer game whose object was the capture and rape of Amerindian women.

Such elements of the tradition, growing in underground darkness or overground sunlight, have undoubtedly helped to nourish the interest shown by the American media in the crimes committed in Juárez, which combine all the most unsettling obsessions of American popular culture: sex, race, money . . . and death.

## ¿Para qué?

*Sadismo m. Placer perverso que se experimenta ante el sufrimiento de otra persona.*
Sadism. Perverse pleasure felt at the suffering of another person.

*Muerte y contribuciones.* Death and taxes. They are, it is said, always with us. *Violación tambien.* So is rape. Every culture recognises it and almost all, ostensibly at least, condemn it under some circumstances. But some women – prostitutes and the very poor – lack the right to deny their bodies, and all women are vulnerable. But why do men rape? Why are women raped?

There is almost certainly no single, simple answer, and any analysis that offers one must fall by that very fact. But just as there is murder and serial murder, so there is rape and serial rape. Some men rape once, and never again, others rape once, and then twice, and then go on raping until they die. Or are caught and jailed. And then, in prison, they may themselves be the targets of rape.

Research has shown that for some rapists, it is the *suffering* of the victim, not the sex of the victim, that is the trigger of arousal. See an experiment described in H.J. Eysenck and D.K.B. Nias' *Sex, Violence and the Media*, in which imprisoned rapists were aroused by suffering, irrespective of sex, and not by consensual sex. This group will have a preferred sex to target, but in its absence they will turn with almost equal readiness to the other. Just so long as there is suffering in the sexual act. Screams. Tears. Bleeding. This is where rape becomes a blood-red amalgam with sadism. The criminal – or criminals – of Juárez add a third ingredient: death. They rape, and then kill. And this is a riddle. Sex was designed to preserve life, not to end it. How does the sexual instinct become so corrupted inside the mind of a criminal that he can take pleasure in the suffering and death of a sexual partner?

This is the riddle of necro-sadism. And perhaps the answer lies, partly, in overcrowding. In *caging*. When animals – mice, rats, monkeys – are forced together in overcrowded cages, their normal instincts become corrupted or disappear entirely. Females eat their young. Strong individuals torment and even kill the weak. Males discard the rituals of mating and force themselves on unwilling partners. Translate these corruptions of natural instinct into human terms and we have – what? We have these things: infanticide; murder; rape.

Juárez is like a cage. Two million human beings are crowded together on a few square kilometres of land. Food, water, and shelter are scarce and must be competed for. There is a struggle for survival that corrupts and then, in some, destroys the instincts we share with the animals, leaving finally only the most powerful one, the most deeply rooted: the instinct of self-preservation. The instinct to preserve and to *gratify* the self. To seek pleasure. And if you can find pleasure in the destruction of another of those individuals who compete with you for survival, all the better. *Matar dos parajos de un tiro*. Kill two birds with one stone.

And in Spanish just as in English, 'bird' can carry two meanings: feathered biped, and female human being. *Pajara* is a term of abuse for a woman – meaning a tart, a slag, a slut. It is a word used by *machistas*, adherents of *machismo*. Like *péon*, *machismo* is a word used in English, and like *péon*, it came into English from the Spanish of México: '*machismo m. Comportamiento del hombre que se cree superior a la mujer.*'

Which means: 'behaviour of the man who believes himself superior to women'. In Spanish, 'to believe' is *creer*, one letter away from *crear*, 'to create'. And the creed of creation is, of course, that man was created first, that woman was created after him and *from* him. Man is superior to woman by Holy Writ. Woman is inferior to man. This is the teaching of Catholicism, which mingles with and reinforces the *machismo* of México until, in a hot, airless atmosphere of overcrowding and struggle for survival, the mixture ferments and turns sour. Juárez is a poisonous laboratory of the soul where acids are mixed in male hearts and then poured out – seething, steaming, flesh-destroying – on female bodies and lives.

Necro-sadism –
'Pleasure from raping PLUS killing the victim.

Overcrowding?
loss /corruption of human instincts?

# 2. Death

*Muerte f. Cesación completa de la vida.*
Death: Complete cessation of life.

'Society is more interested in a death than in a life.' (Dennis Nilsen, as reported in Brian Masters' *Killing for Company*, p. 183, 1995, Arrow Books)

July dusk in the desert outside Juárez. It is intensely quiet but there is movement, the nocturnal shift of macro- and microfauna taking over from the diurnal. Scorpio is rising on the western horizon. A meteor scratches a brief red line into the face of the zenith, and as though this were a signal a sound begins to bleed into the silence. The sound of an engine. It gets louder quickly, swelling in time with a splash of yellow light in the west that bleaches out Scorpio. The engine noise and the yellow light are coming from a pick-up bumping its way along a little-used road. The movement in the desert has stopped, broken like the silence. Everything is waiting. Music mingles with the engine noise now – fast, up-beat *norteña* from a local station (*norteña* is a form of contemporary folk music characteristic of northern México). When the pick-up stops and the engine is switched off the music carries on, fanning out into the silence and stillness. In the time it has taken for the pick-up to drive out here and stop, dusk has turned into night.

Someone gets out of the driver's seat of the pick-up, leaving the door open. It is a man, dressed in jeans and open-necked shirt. Thick-set, medium height. He walks to the rear of the pick-up and takes down the backboard, tugs a heavy tarpaulin and layers of cloth off a pale heap of something and drags it out. It falls heavily to the desert floor and lies there. The man walks back to the driver's seat, gets in, closes the door, starts the engine up. His arm is hanging out of the window now, banging the door in time to the music as he turns the pick-up and drives back the way he came, hardly bothering to avoid the heap of pale something he left lying on the sand.

It is a naked corpse. A woman in her late teens or early twenties, slender, long hair forming a darker pool of shadow around her head as the headlights of the pick-up pass disinterestedly over her. As the pick-up gets further away Scorpio begins to shine again through the diminishing yellow splash of its headlights, contributing in time to the starshine that just allows her face to be seen. It is swollen, darker than her body, staring up into the sky with unnaturally protuberant eyes. She has been strangled (*complete fracture of the hyoid*, a pathologist might write if her body is discovered in time) and raped (*severe bruising of the labia majora et minora; laceration of the fourchette*). Her legs fell apart as she was dumped and the starshine is glistening on something wet between them. Blood (*O rhesus negative*) and semen (*non-secretor*). Her breasts are gazing blindly up into the sky too (*multiple bruising and scratches*) with dark, blood-encrusted nipples (*base of left mammilla partly bitten through*).

Free of the tarpaulin and cloth she is starting to cool, her bruised and cut skin starting the drop to ambient temperature. There is movement in the desert again. Small eyes and nostrils, smaller antennae, are examining her, interpreting her, dismissing her. Barely 30 m off and 5 m up, however, there are eyes and nostrils that would be very interested in her indeed, only they are switched off for the night. The shapes of their owners can be seen (*Coragyps atratus*, to an ornithologist), hunched against the star-field of Libra atop the blunter, taller shapes of cactus (*Pachycereus pringlei*, to a botanist).

A snake (*Crotalus atrox*) swims by across the sand, scales whispering on the harshness of its grains. The infrared sensors in its head-pits pick out her limbs and torso against the fading background of solar heat and it pauses a second, contemplating a final meal, before realising that the heat-shapes are parts of a larger whole, too large to eat, and dead anyway. It glides on its way, heading for its hole. A few minutes later a scorpion (*Buthus mexicanus*), attracted too by the lingering traces of heat in her skin, climbs atop her right foot. It pauses, seeming to salute its astrological namesake with raised claws, discovers similarly that she is dead, and climbs off.

Then she is left alone beneath the stars. Scorpio reaches its zenith and begins the long fall into the west. Hours pass. The movement increases around her, the nocturnal shift of fauna heading for their holes and lairs, the first representatives of the diurnal shift emerging from theirs. The sky begins to pale in the east. The dark shapes of the *Coragyps atratus* begin to move, heads shifting and peering dimly around them. In another half an hour they will have seen her. It is dusk again, almost exactly twelve hours after she was dumped. Her skin is at ambient temperature now and she is invisible to snakes and scorpions until the sun rises fully. Dusk gives way to twilight, twilight to dawn. The shapes atop the *Pachycereus pringlei* have seen her. They shuffle from foot to foot then take to the air, flapping their wings a few times before relaxing, legs hanging, into the long glide that will land them within easy waddling and hopping distance of her. What was it they were called again? *Coragyps atratus*. Black vultures.

# 3. Life

*Vida f. Conjunto de los fenómenos que concurren al desarrollo y la conservacion de los seres orgánicos.*

Life. The set of phenomena that underlie the development and preservation of organic beings.

'The Nightmare *Life-in-Death* was she . . .' [*The Rime of the Ancient Mariner*, Samuel Taylor Coleridge (1772–1834)]

She had been conceived seventeen years and eighty-six days before on 3 July 1981 in a small town outside Coatzacoalcos in Vera Cruz, a province in south-eastern México. Her parents were newly married, her father working as a fisherman on the Gulf of México, often absent for weeks at a time, her mother as a loom-tender in an American-owned textiles factory. She was born on 14 March 1982, a little prematurely. Her mother was back at work four days later, and had difficulty getting time off to attend the christening, where the new-born girl-child was given the names Elena Lidia Matilda Arriaga: Elena for her paternal grandmother, Lidia for her mother's favourite aunt, Matilda for her natal saint.

She was a quiet baby, large-eyed, watchful, and rarely complaining, even at the occasional hunger she experienced when money was shorter than usual. Her mother left her during work hours at the home of a great-aunt, a pious, superstitious woman prone to bouts of drinking and tears, but mostly conscientious in her childminding at other times. The aunt sometimes wondered, amusing the child with a swinging rosary over the cradle, whether this latest of her grandnieces would die quite soon – for she had lost three of her own children, and they had all been quiet and easy to manage, sliding quickly down the dark slopes of disease and malnutrition towards death.

But Elena did not die. Not then. She remained quiet, learning to talk early but rarely using the words she gathered with feminine facility from the lips and tongues of those around her. Another child was born to her parents at the end of the same year, a boy, Hernando, and she seemed content to stay in the shadow cast over her by his noisy, demanding exuberance. By the age of three, she was helping her mother with the care of her younger brother and of the two sisters, María-José, and Conchita, who had been born after him (a further child, another boy, had died in a local epidemic of *sarampión* – measles). Shortly after her fourth birthday, her mother died in a bus crash and her father had to migrate north for work, leaving his four motherless children in the care of the great-aunt. After a year, money stopped arriving from the north, and they never heard from him again, nor ever learned what had happened to him.

She was six before she first attended school, quick to learn, mostly unnoticed by the teachers, but always there to be called upon to teach or comfort a younger child in difficulty. She was often absent, increasingly so during her second and third years, but the school knew of the circumstances at home, with her great-aunt sliding finally into full-blown alcoholism, and no comments were made. Despite her absences she had no difficulties with the work and had she been from a wealthier family she would have been marked already for *universidad* and a career, perhaps, as a bilingual secretary in México City or even Miami or Los Angeles, the zenith of ambition for a peasant girl from a poor region of a poor country.

But the prospect was never mentioned to her, because of course it was almost impossible, and the teachers judged it better to say nothing. They had seen many like her come and go, a few more brilliant, and knew her absences would increase and lengthen until finally she would, unofficially, have left school for good and people would start to forget the thin, quiet girl in clean but shabby clothes who sat on the left of the class, in the sunshine. Once, when she had impressed a rare government inspector with a quick answer to a question, her teacher made a note to give her advice, even offer her help with finding tuition in English, the golden key to advancement, but she was absent the next day, and the next, and the next, and every day after that. She had, unofficially, left school, aged thirteen-and-a-half, and people quickly started to forget her.

She had left because she had found a job gutting fish at one of the canning firms by the harbour. She had lied about her age, and the man who hired her knew she had lied, but young workers would work harder for less and he was happy to take her on. The job was dirty – stinking – and the smock she wore turned stiff with fish-blood and scales and the sinews and muscles in her wrists and fingers sang with agony for an hour after she finished in the evening. But she needed the money.

For by then her great-aunt was dying in a free hospital run by the Church, and her brother and two sisters were at school. One, Conchita, was doing almost as well as her eldest sister before her, and the hopes of the motherless, fatherless family were centred on her. Hernando, nearing thirteen, slow but strong, wanted to leave school and find work too, but Elena was trying to persuade him to stay on a couple more years, fearful that with money of his own he would fall into drugs, or glue-sniffing. He did not. He did not have time. Like his mother, he was killed in a crash, travelling in a car with friends, late at night. The car had been stolen, but the police made no trouble, for it had been too burnt and twisted by the crash to be recognisable to them or its owner.

In the year after the crash, aged fourteen-and-a-half, Elena managed to find a better job in the warehouse of a *supermercado*, a supermarket. After a week or two she was initiated by older workers into the pilfering that had gone on there for years. She was reluctant, and would only take food, but it helped save a little money for birthdays and for Conchita and her school books. The job lasted two years and then she was sacked with half the rest of the warehouse staff when a new manager arrived and decided on a show of zeal and honesty before reorganising the theft on a more systematic and profitable scale.

Five years into NAFTA – The North American Free Trade Agreement, much criticised in México for lowering wages and destroying jobs – work was hard to find in Vera Cruz, and she had two months of unemployment before she decided to leave the province and travel north to find a job in the *maquiladora* corridor. She was not sure at first which city to try, but she still remembered her mother telling her about the revolutions in the nineteenth century, and the role played in them by Benito Juárez, so she chose the city named after him (she rarely had the money or the time to buy newspapers or watch the *televisión*, so she did not know that Juárez was becoming famous for another reason than its revolutionary namesake). She had to borrow money for the trip and though she found a job almost at once on her arrival in Ciudad Juárez, her first month's wages went on paying off the debt. Then she was able to start sending money directly to Conchita and María, living on as little as possible herself and trying to resist the demands of the new friends she had made that she stop thinking eternally of others and enjoy herself a little. One Tuesday she won something on a twenty-five-peso lottery ticket and went out with her friends to enjoy herself a little.

She was not at work the next day, and the next, and the next, or on any day after that. The cheques stopped arriving in the small town outside Coatzacoalcos, Vera Cruz province, south-eastern México. María and Conchita never heard from her again, nor ever learned what had happened to her. Only the man in the pick-up, and the black vultures, ever knew that.

# 4. Work

*Trabajo m. (1) Ocupación retribuida. En economía política, uno de los factores de la producción. (2) Fenómenos que se producen en una sustancia y cambian su naturaleza o su forma: trabajo de descomposición.*

Work. (1) Paid occupation. In political economy, one of the factors of production. (2) Phenomena that are produced in a substance and change its nature or form: *the work of decomposition.*

'*Facito aliquid operis, ut semper te diabolus inveniat occupatum*'. 'Keep working at something, that the devil might always find thee occupied.' [St Jerome (?347–?420 AD)]

The Latin word for enjoyment or leisure is *otium*, and the opposite of enjoyment is *neg-otium*, business or work. This is an attitude that has lingered in the cultures founded and still influenced by the Romans: those of France and Spain, for example, where 'work' is *travaille* and *trabajo* respectively. The words have a common root, and the French is still close to the English travail, meaning 'painful or excessive labour or exertion'. All three words ultimately come from a Vulgar Latin word meaning 'to torture', *tripaliare*, from the older Latin *trepalium*, an instrument of torture constructed of *tres pali*, three stakes, to which the victim was bound for the attentions of the torturer and his instruments.

In most of the Western world, such a simile – that work is akin to torture – could only be used jocularly or with conscious hyperbole. Work is hard for most people in the West, but it does not usually shorten life and irrevocably destroy health. It can be boring, frustrating, unpleasant, stressful . . . but painful? Agonising? Not in most people's experience. Not in the West. It is often very different in the Third World, and México is part of the Third World. Work there can often be compared to torture without jocularity, without any trace of humour other than the blackest. In México work often shortens lives and destroys health. That is one of the reasons work has been created there by companies from the United States and other countries in the rich West. In México these companies

19

need not concern themselves or their shareholders with such niceties as workers' rights, unless the workers in question are valuable to the company.

The latter is not true of those who work on assembly lines, needing only a clear eye and a steady hand, but it is of those who work to design or invent what those who work on the assembly lines will assemble. These designers and inventors need to have something special, something that – unlike clear eyes and steady hands – cannot easily be found and bought. Abdul Latif Sharif Sharif was one of those who had this special something. It had already helped him find well-paid work long before he arrived in México to work for a *maquiladora* in Ciudad Juárez. It also helped him retain the work he found when he was accused of rape and violent assaults on women:

> Sharif was a scientist of inventive genius. US companies stood to make millions from his work and helped find for their problematic employee the finest legal defense available. One Midland, Texas, company hired him from prison, helped him avoid deportation to Egypt, and stood by him as evidence of his terrible nature mounted. ('MONSTER' BEATS THE SYSTEM, Tim Madigan, The *Seattle Times*, 1999)

Before then, in 1981, while living in Palm Beach, Florida, Sharif was accused of rape and assault by a young woman called Tracey, who said she had been given drugged vodka when invited by Sharif to his apartment for a party that turned out to be a *tête-à-tête*. He denied the charges:

> Jim Gambale, the owner of Cercoa Inc. and Sharif's boss, was inclined to believe him. Sharif had been fired from his last job in New Jersey. Something about a padded expense account. But no one questioned Sharif's genius in the laboratory, a chemist who, in the words of one colleague, 'could make a bomb out of Bisquick' [a biscuit mix popular in the United States]. Sharif was a great guy. He was being railroaded. It was Gambale who helped

Sharif find and pay for the highly regarded Palm Beach defense lawyer, Greg Scott. (*Ibid.*, The *Seattle Times*)

Sharif avoided any serious consequences from this escapade, but ended up in prison shortly afterwards as a result of a nearly identical crime, when, after moving to a new job in Gainesville, Florida, he raped and assaulted a young woman called Lisa on her first night in his apartment as a live-in housekeeper. He was sentenced to twelve years' imprisonment on 31 January 1984, but was out a little less than six years later in October 1989. He walked from prison straight into another well-paid job, this time for Benchmark Research and Technology, an oil company in Midland, Texas. Patents from this period can be found with his name on them in the archives of the US Patents Office, evidence that Sharif's expertise was earning large sums for Sharif himself, and large sums for the company he worked for.

Which, yet again, was prepared to stand by him and back him with the best lawyers when he fell foul of the law once more. The machinery of the US Immigration service had finally begun to move, for Sharif had already committed enough crimes to be deported. A deportation hearing belatedly got underway in El Paso, Texas. The judge finally ordered him deported, but his lawyers immediately appealed and Sharif was released on bail. On Hallowe'en night, 1993, he met a woman called Ann in a nightclub in his old haunt of Midland:

He talked her into visiting his home that night, then trapped her there, raping her again and again until the sun came up. There were moments when Ann wondered whether she would live to see her children. (*Ibid.*, The *Seattle Times*)

As pointed out elsewhere, the period of Sharif's bail is likely to have been his first prolonged acquaintance with the pleasures available to a man of his tastes in Juárez, just across the Rio Grande from El Paso. Having liked what he experienced in Juárez, Sharif went into voluntary exile there when he was charged with the rape of Ann. In Juárez he took up yet another well-paid job working in a *maquiladora* for Benchmark, and started, the authorities now believe, on the career of rape and serial murder that would see him behind bars yet again, this time seemingly for good in a Mexican prison.

But for Sharif, life in the gritty city neighboring El Paso would be more Eden than exile, at least at first. Most of the city's two million residents lived in wretched poverty, tens of thousands in cardboard shacks with no electricity or running water. Sharif's home, by comparison, was a spacious two-storey Spanish-style villa with stucco walls and tile roof. He was a brilliant chemist who joined the Juárez gentry of doctors, lawyers, architects and drug lords. (*Ibid.*, The *Seattle Times*)

But Sharif, living there at the apex of the pyramid of work, was more than willing to descend regularly to those at the base of the same pyramid. Young women were preferred for jobs at the lowest levels because, as one BBC report on the crimes put it, 'they tend to be more dextrous and less bolshy than the men'. The report then went on to give an additional reason: young women, without children, still living with their parents, want money to enjoy themselves:

After all week on the factory floor, on Friday night they dress up and go out to the discos. It's their only way to stay sane. Standing in skimpy tops, laughing together they tell you that the small amount of money they earn is for themselves to spend as they want. (Tom Carver, 'Mexico's murder town', BBC, 9 September 1999)

This pursuit of pleasure brought the *maquiladora* workers of Sharif's day into the same environment that, as we have already seen from his meeting with the rape victim Ann, Sharif habitually stalked: the nightclubs and bars of a teeming city centre. In Juárez, nightclubs and bars are most heavily concentrated, as is to be expected, in the central district, and

to any present-day inhabitant of the city only three syllables
have to be spoken to conjure them: *oo-gaar-tê*. Ugarte:

> Hundreds of rickety buses rumbled onto Ugarte around
> the clock, depositing thousands of naïve teenage girls with
> painted nails and fresh lipstick. They were part of the
> legion of workers in foreign-owned factories, the
> *maquiladoras*, girls who made three dollars a day, then
> stepped from their buses downtown and virtually onto the
> laps of men who bore them ill. ('MONSTER' BEATS THE SYSTEM,
> Tim Madigan, The *Seattle Times*, 1999)

It seems very difficult to doubt that among these men was
a well-groomed, well-dressed, charismatic, charming, highly
intelligent serial-killer called Abdul Latif Sharif Sharif. Sharif
was as good at both his day job and his night one as a
well-groomed, well-dressed, charismatic, charming, intelligent serial killer called Peter Sutcliffe had once been. When
Sutcliffe took a job as a lorry-driver with a family haulage firm
called Clark's near Bradford, northern England:

> Tom Clark and his son William were soon to overcome
> any reservations they had about taking on an
> inexperienced new driver. The new man was quiet and
> polite and kept the most perfect records they had ever
> seen . . . Very conscientious; a pity all the drivers weren't
> like him. Four months later, on 5 February 1977,
> Sutcliffe took Irene Richardson to Soldiers (*sic*) Field,
> Roundhay Park, Leeds, hit her three times over the head
> with a hammer, and slashed and stabbed her stomach so
> badly her intestines spilled out. (*The Yorkshire Ripper: an
> in-depth study of a mass killer and his methods*, Roger
> Cross, p. 71, HarperCollins, 1993)

Ciudad Juárez, northern México, would soon be subject to
the same bloody reign of terror in the 1990s as the towns of
northern England had been in the 1970s and 1980s.

# 5. Juárez

*Ciudad Juárez, c. de México (Chihuahua), puerto en el río Bravo. Industrias. Comercio. Universidad. Obispado.*

Juárez City, city in México (Chihuahua state), port on the Rio Grande. Industries. University. Bishopric.

Sandwiches. Boycotts. And chihuahuas. Sandwiches are more famous than the man – an eighteenth-century English aristocrat – who gave them their name, as are boycotts. Chihuahuas were named not for a man but for a state. Chihuahua is the largest state in México, and sprawls across thousands of square kilometres of desert and mountain, from the borders with the American states of Texas and New México down almost as far as the Pacific coast across from the Mexican state of Baja California.

And the largest city in the largest state in México is Ciudad Juárez. Literally 'Juárez City', named in 1888 for a Mexican political hero, the rebel-leader Benito Juárez (1806–72). Previously it had been known as *El Paso del Norte*: North Pass. For Juárez has always been most famous as a place not to go to, but to go *through*: a crossing-place uniting a convenient mountain pass with a convenient ford of the Río Bravo. And when, after the Mexican–American war of 1847–8, the river became a border, splitting the region in two between a waning México and a waxing America, Juárez itself was split in two: half, on the southern bank of the Bravo, remaining Mexican, half, on the northern, becoming American.

This American half still preserves part of the old, undivided city's name: El Paso. El Paso, Texas, one half-automatically completes, for the city is not particularly populous or famous. Except, perhaps, as a border-crossing, a gateway for Americans to Mexican 'food, shopping, nightlife'. And women. Mexican goods, and Mexican women, are exotic. And cheap:

The whores are out, sixteen- and seventeen-year-olds.
There is no way to tell if they are full-time prostitutes or
factory workers making an extra buck. The peso has lost
another chunk of its value in the last day or so.

'How much?' I ask.

She leans into the car window and says the equivalent
of fourteen dollars.

'How long?' I say.

'How long can you resist me?' she asks with a laugh.
('While You Were Sleeping', Charles Bowden, *Harper's*
magazine, December 1996)

Juárez could be regarded as a kind of contact sore, a
purulent wound ground out on the border by the rubbing
together of American plutocracy and Mexican poverty, of
American desire and Mexican desperation. Earlier in the
century Tijuana, another city split in two by the post-bellum
realignment of México and the United States, had been
another kind of contact sore:

In describing how Carpophorus trained the animals that
had relations with women, I used Apuleius and also the
technique employed by the Mexican gentleman I met in
Tia Juana (*sic*) who was making 16 mm stag films on the
subject. (*Those About to Die*, Daniel Mannix, Panther,
London, 1960)

For decades Mexican women have been selling their bodies
and their dignity like this in northern border cities, withhold-
ing only one thing: their lives. These they will not and cannot
exchange for American dollars, and so these have to be taken
by force. And *can* be taken by force – and with far greater ease
than those of their sisters, white or Latina, in the United
States.

These facts have flowed down the gutters and conduits of
culture in the United States to create a reeking sludge where
American perceptions of México and Mexican women have
seeded some startlingly poisonous swamp-flowers of heterosexual male fantasy:

Down in Cunt Valley where Red Rivers flow,
Where cocksuckers flourish and whoremongers grow,
There lives a young maiden that I do adore
She's my Hot Fuckin' Cocksuckin' Mexican whore.

CHORUS

Oh Lupe, Lupe, dead in her tomb,
While maggots crawl out of her decomposed womb.
But the smile on her face is a mute cry for more!
She's my Hot Fuckin' Cocksuckin' Mexican whore.

This is one of a number of songs from an unofficial rugby song website – more follow below. The date given for the song is 1980, but the song itself is, however, doubtless at least a few decades older, for the ready sexual availability of Mexican women on which it predicates its necrophiliac stanzas has long been an important component of heterosexual male American folk knowledge, and can also be found in the most famous of all obscene drinking songs in the English language, 'Eskimo Nell'.

Eskimos are, of course, Amerindians, and so are part of the white male erotic obsession with the dark female, but at the time described by the song Nell is working as a prostitute not in the north but in the south. From internal evidence, it could even be suggested that she plies her trade in Juárez, for the song's anti-heroes 'Mexican Pete' and 'Dead-eye Dick' head south to their nemesis. In the website version their journey is described like this:

So do or dare this horny pair,
Set forth for the Rio Grande [i.e. the Mexican–American border],
Dead-eye Dick with his mighty ***** (*sic*)
And Pete with his gun in his hand.

'At the height of a blazing noon', they enter a saloon-cum-brothel whose male clientele are 'dagos' and order 'forty whores', presumably also 'dago', to strip:

Now Dead-eye Dick was breathing quick
With lecherous snorts and grunts
As forty ***** were bared to view
And likewise forty *****.

Now forty ***** and forty *****
If you can use your wits,
And if you're slick at arithmetic,
Makes exactly eighty tits. (*Ibid., sic omnia.*)


'Maria', a lesser-known song, makes the Mexican *mise en scène* even more explicit:

Maria, Maria, she's got gonorrhoea,
She gave it to me, amigo,
Oh my amigo,
I will visit the doctor today.

CHORUS

Ay yai, yai, yai,
Si, si senora (*sic*),
Tra la, la la, la la la la la,
Tra la, la la, la la la.


This association of *Méxicanas* – Mexican women – with disease and corruption is reinforced even further in the second verse when a woman called Melinda is described as urinating from a window on to a *sombrero*, the archetypal piece of Mexican headwear. Such songs are known as 'rugby songs' in the United Kingdom and other white nations of its Commonwealth, and yet the two examples given here, with many others in the canon, are clearly imported from the United States. One can only conclude that Mexican women have long figured in the fantasies and sex-tourism of American men, and there is, indeed, evidence that they have done so at least as far back as the nineteenth century. They have, however, become even more prominent in American fantasy and sex-tourism in the final decade of the twentieth century, as the population of México has been forced to unprecedented levels of mobility in the search for work. Many thousands of Mexican women have headed and are heading north to the *maquiladora* corridor, young, naïve, alone, losing contact with family and friends in the south, taking a succession of short-term jobs in huge factories and assembly plants, and so becoming ideal prey for serial killers. Certain questions inevitably arise. How many women have disappeared who have never even been recorded as *desconocidas* – unknown female victims – because their bodies have never been found? Whose bodies have never even been searched for, because no one knew they had ever gone missing?

And was knowledge of this killing ground under construction in Juárez what brought Sharif south in the early nineties? In emigrating, after all, he could exchange an American criminal record and the vigilance of the rich, well-resourced, forensically sophisticated American police for the anonymity of a cancerously growing Mexican border city and an overburdened, under-resourced, forensically primitive police force that was unaware of his past.

If so, he was an appropriate figure to take his place in the *Comedia de Terrores*, the Comedy of Terrors, about to play itself out in Juárez under the gaze of the American media. Another aspect of the American relationship with México is its being not just a place to travel *to* but also a place to travel *from*. México is the last stage in a journey from poor, Roman Catholic Latin America to the rich, Protestant United States. But this journey is not undertaken just by people, but also by goods and animals. Goods and animals that are, like people, unwanted by the United States. As the song 'Maria' has already suggested, a constant image of México presented in the American media is that of a source of infection and contamination: the infection and contamination of drugs and of almost Biblical plagues of animals:

Natives of the upper Paraguay River floodplain where Brazil, Argentina, and Paraguay meet, red fire ants (*Solenopsis invicta*) first [appeared in the United States] in the 1930s. They soon proved to be among the insect world's fastest and fiercest colonisers ... A mound can be up to a yard high and five feet in diameter, linked to a wider tunnel system and housing hundreds of thousands of ants ... Children have died from multiple bites [and, in] infested areas, between thirty and sixty per cent of the population are stung each year. (*Why Things Bite Back*, Edward Tenner, p. 111, Fourth Estate, London, 1996)

'Infested areas' of the United States are mostly those that have borders with México. An even more famous Mexican emigrant to the United States is, however, a species whose arrival was anticipated with dread for more than two decades. One of the earliest examinations of the threat it posed coupled it explicitly with other famous Latin American exports:

The banana boat *Cubahama* ... Six a.m. on a humid August morning ... A US Customs launch idled off the port stern, watching for any suspicious activity ... The Customs Bureau had been tipped off that there would almost certainly be cocaine on board [but] this time the contraband would not be cocaine ... At seven a.m. sharp, the US Customs team boarded the *Cubahama* ... Inspector Denis Bracken jumped down inside [the hold]. Suddenly there was a scream and a loud buzzing sound ... Bracken was waving his arms frantically and running wildly, trampling boxes of bananas ... Captain Paul Keough, who was in charge of the search party, ran to Bracken, now lying face down in the hold ... He turned [him] over to try mouth-to-mouth resuscitation, but drew back in horror.

Bracken's face was swollen to twice its normal size and marked with huge red welts. His lips were bulbous, grotesque. As Keough opened Bracken's mouth he saw [the killers] crawling on his tongue and down his throat. They had flown into Bracken's mouth when he screamed for help. (*The Killer Bees*, Anthony Potter, p. 1, Grosset & Dunlap, New York, 1977.)

Three Latin American exports are here combined in one narrative: bananas, cocaine, and a deadly hybrid species of *Apis mellifera* that is notorious throughout the world as the 'killer bee' and that was created in Brazil by cross-breeding of native species with an aggressive import from Africa. Although fans of the late Peter Cook might find killer bees more laughable than frightening, they are in fact no joking matter for inhabitants of the regions they breed in, and would be better called not *Apis mellifera*, the 'honey-bearing bee', but *Apis letifera*, 'the death-bearing bee'.

And yet the narrative just quoted is fiction, a scene from a journalist's imagination presenting how the first citizen of the United States to die at the stingers of this new Latin American export might do so. Bananas . . . Cocaine . . . Killer bees . . . All implicit, deliberate, designed references to the origins of the threat. Non-fiction refers to the origins of the threat not contrivedly, but contingently, and yet is even more explicit:

> After futile efforts to create Central American barrier zones, more African bees were found near Hidalgo, Texas, in October 1990. In July three years later, an eighty-two-year-old farmer, the first US casualty of the invaders, died from dozens of stings after poking the wrong beehive with a stick in an abandoned house in the border town of Rio Grande City, Texas. (*Why Things Bite Back*, Edward Tenner, p. 134, Fourth Estate, London, 1996)

'Hidalgo' . . . 'Rio Grande City' . . . 'Border town' . . . After these references, the origin of these alien, killer bees hardly needs setting out in cold print. Texas – a Mexican name truncated and remarried to its origins in the culinary and cultural adjective 'Tex-Mex' – accounts for more than half of México's border with the United States, and there is a better than even chance that any unwanted 'invader' making its way north from Latin America will appear first in Texas, having crossed directly from México.

The association of México with death and suffering is, then, a long-standing element of American perceptions of their southern neighbour, lying eternally ready to be fanned into crackling, fuming life by new reports of some deadly aspect of Mexican life or culture, such as the crimes being committed in the border city of Juárez. And yet it is possible to question whether the reports of rape and sex murder that began to filter out of México were new to *all* the citizens of the United States.

# 6. Rebels

*Rebelde adj. y s. Que se rebela. Que se niega a obedecer a la autoridad legitima.*
Rebel(lious). Noun (and adjective). One who rebels. One who refuses to obey
legitimate authority.

The word 'rebellion' has a strong taste in the mouth,
sometimes sweet, sometimes bitter, for the speakers of any
language, but particularly for speakers of Mexican Spanish.
The very existence of México was won by rebellion, the rights
of her people fought for and sustained by it, her heroes and
folk myths forged and tempered by it. The taste of rebellion
is sweet in Mexican mouths, and sweet in Mexican reality.
Above all in the north, in the state of Chihuahua, whose hero
of heroes is Francisco 'Pancho' Villa (1877–1923), bandit,
womaniser, and rebel.

Something of all this must have been in the minds of a
group of youths from Juárez when they formed a gang and
chose the name for it. The name they chose was *Los Rebeldes*
– The Rebels. *Los que se niegan a obedecer a la autoridad
legitima* – those who refuse to obey legitimate authority. But
that is a definition from a Spanish dictionary in both senses:
a dictionary of Spanish published in Spain. One published in
México might not stress that authority was legitimate. And
anyway, it is better 'to reign in hell, than serve in heav'n'.
Particularly when the hell you reign in is self-created, and you
are not the one to suffer in it.

Juan Jorge Contreras Jurado, 'El Grande' – 'Big Guy' – was
twenty-three years old when he made his declaration at
10:30 a.m. on 15 April 1996.

'El Grande' said he was a worker in a *maquiladora* and came
from San Pedro de las Colonias, Coahuila state.

In his declaration, the detained man confesses to being a
member of the gang of *Los Rebeldes* and gives a detailed
account of his participation in the crimes committed in Lomas
de Poleo, Juárez.

The following is part of his testimony that forms part of the investigation undertaken by Judge Quinto de lo Penal:

'The first Saturday in March, 1996, at three in the morning, I was inside the dance hall La Tuna, located on Ugarte Street, drinking a beer, when El Diablo – "The Devil" – and Carlos Barrientos Vidales, alias "Charly the Dancer", came in.

'A short while after, El Sinaloa, also known as "El Chapito", came in, and later José Luis Reyes came in.

'I said to El Chapito or El Sinaloa, or maybe to Carlos Armando Molina Mariscal, that I was off back home, to which he said, okay, and so we all went off in a Ford LTD Crown Victoria.

'But because Carlos Armando Molina Mariscal, who was driving, did not go in the direction of my house, I asked them why they were not taking me home.

'El Diablo told me that first they were going for money to his girlfriend's place. The only thing I knew about her was that she was the dancer in the Faustos bar but now I know that she called herself Lucy and lived in the hotel Río de Janeiro. Later when we got to the hotel, El Diablo and Charly the Dancer got out of the car and went into the hotel and came back after about ten minutes.

'I saw that Charly the Dancer was carrying Lucy in his arms and that she was tied up and gagged and because of that I got out of the car with the intention of getting away but, when he saw me doing this, El Diablo said to me, "We're going to have some fun with her and if you do not come I will sort you out."

'We drove off down Mariscal Street going from north to south, till we came to where they sell snacks for a *peso*. Maybe before we got to Ugarte Street, we came across Héctor, who has only got one leg and who I now know is called Héctor Raymundo Olivares Villalba.

'El Diablo threatens him, saying, "Get in or I will sort you out," so Héctor got into the car in the back seat, staying on the left-hand side.

'El Diablo said to El Chapita, "Go that way," meaning the Anapra side of the street. We were getting drugged up with cocaine at the time.

'El Diablo used one of his fingers to try and make Lucy take some coke, but she did not want to and pushed herself to one side, so El Diablo does not make a fuss about it and snorts the cocaine that he had on his finger.

'On the drive, El Diablo said to us, "When we get there we are going to rape her," so I asked why and El Diablo said to me not to be a coward.

'When we got there, Charly the Dancer got Lucy out and El Diablo immediately pushed him off her, like the two of them had got out of the car straight away, and then they put her on the ground, face-up.

'Charly unbuttons her pants, which were a kind of whitish tweed colour, and pulls them off her and then takes off her blouse and pulls her knickers down one of her legs.

'Lucy was half-conscious and El Diablo dropped his pants and his underpants past his knees and then got on top of Lucy, opened her legs, and then he raped her.

'Because Lucy struggled, El Diablo started to hit her with his fists until she stopped struggling, and he stayed penetrating her for about fifteen or twenty minutes.

'After El Diablo finished, Charly the Dancer and El Chapito did the same.

'After they had both finished, El Diablo said to me, "Fuck her as well, do not be an arsehole," so I dropped my pants and underpants, but I turned Lucy face-down and grabbed hold of her waist and she stayed face-down and that was how I raped her.

'El Diablo, when he saw that I had finished, came up to me and said, "Get off her, I am going to fuck her again."

'Then El Diablo started to strangle her and we all got into the car.

'El Diablo was the last to get into the car. He got behind the wheel and we asked him about Lucy, so he said to us, "She has been sorted out," so I asked him why he had done it and he told me that, "There will not be any hassle, she does not have any relatives."

'He [got out again and] stayed there to deal with Lucy's body and the rest of us went back the way we had come. We left Héctor on the corner of Mariscal and Ugarte Street and I got out at the Cathedral. I also want to say that about a year and a half before I was introduced by Sergio Armendáriz Díaz, El Diablo, to someone who he said was called George, who I went on seeing and hanging out with there sometimes. I have found out now that he is an Egyptian and is called Sharif Sharif, and about a month ago I went to visit him in the Centre of Adult Rehabilitation, better known as the *CeReSo*, and he gave me an envelope of money and told me to give it to El Diablo.

'I also want to say that I went to see George, or Sharif Sharif, because El Diablo threatened me. He said, "Go and see George and pick up a packet. If you do not do it, I will sort you and your wife out, because I know where you live. When you get to the *CeReSo* read this bit of paper and say that your name is what is on it, everything is sorted out."

'I do not remember what name I used to get into the *CeReSo*. I went there and picked up the envelope and then went to the Marimar pool hall, on Ugarte Street, where I had already arranged to meet El Diablo at five in the afternoon, and that is what happened. When I handed over the envelope of money to El Diablo, he opened it and put the money in a bag and I saw that it was in one-hundred-dollar bills, and I reckoned up that there was about four thousand dollars.

'When I gave the money to El Diablo he said, "Okay, get lost," and I went straight home to see that my family was alright.' n.b.: Some words in the original text of this and the following confession have been changed because of the coarseness of the descriptions and out of respect for the reader. The text issued by the Public Ministry was also changed for publication in a newspaper, with due regard to its content.

The member of *Los Rebeldes* known as 'El Mocho' described the murder of Rosario García Leal, whose case was the one that allowed the police to establish the identity of the suspects. Héctor Raymundo Oliveres Villalba, 'El Mocho', was born in Ciudad Juárez and at the time of his arrest was working as a singer in dance halls in the city centre. The file created by the Office of Preliminary Investigations states that he was eighteen years old at the time of his statement, but afterwards his family proved that he was a minor and he was released.

'I am a member of the gang called "The Rebels" who come together in [clubs in] the city centre, most often in Tuna, Joe's Place, Fiesta, Divers, and Gilbert's, sometimes in Alive.

'The time I am telling you about, the sixth of December, 1995, a person who I now know is called Juan Jorge Contreras Jurado, alias "El Grande", told me between nine and eleven in the evening that he had been the same day to the *CeReSo* [the detention centre in Juárez] and had a meeting with someone called Sharif by arrangement with a guard, the two of them giving the guard I do not know how much.

'Next day I was outside the Tuna club, in Ugarte Street, next to Copel [a shop], in the city-centre, it would have been sometime between eight and nine in the evening. A white car stopped there, an Oldsmobile, a four-door, with tinted windows and an antenna on the boot shaped like a boomerang or airplane, with El Grande; El Diablo, who I now know is called Sergio Armendáriz Díaz; Charly (*sic*) El Chero; Fernando 'Ferna' Rubén Guermes Aguirre; Gerardo 'El Gera' Fernández Molina; as well as someone else whose name and nickname I did not know, but I now know that he is called José Luis, on board.

'The person behind the steering wheel was José Luis, with me next to him, and next to me Gerardo or "El Flaco". In the back behind the driver was El Grande, with Charly in the middle, and El Diablo next to him.

'I also want to say that on the floor in the back of the car there was a girl who had her mouth gagged and her hands tied behind her back, so that it looked as if she was handcuffed, but she really had her hands tied with a shoe-lace, because she had the shoe-lace missing from one of her shoes, and she could not speak, she could only try to speak or shout.

'I asked El Diablo what the hell was going on and then he told me that we were only going to have a bit of a chat-up "over there", meaning Anapra [a district of Juárez].

On the drive there all the guys were snorting cocaine and after about an hour and twenty minutes' driving, Charly tried to make the girl take some, like with his forefinger and thumb he wanted to put the stuff up her nose, but the girl would not let him, so the guys were hitting her.

'José Luis went on driving without saying where, except that before there had been this fried-chicken stall and I knew the area now. When the car stopped, Gera got out and went to the boot and I do not know what he took out, because just then I went to the front of the car to urinate and the lights of the car were off, which meant the place was very dark.

'Next José Luis got out, and Grande and Charly, and then they pulled the girl to the middle of the seat and turned her face upwards and lifted her legs, and while I got out to urinate they started to take her clothes off.

'Once she was stripped they lifted her legs and José Luis held her underneath, just above her knees, and with his male member out and erect. Then he started to put his hands underneath a dark blouse she was wearing and stroked her breasts and put his member into her.

'Then José Luis spent about fifteen minutes raping her, while the rest of us told him he should stop pestering her.

'Then, once José Luis was finished, Charly came up, dropped his pants below his shins, and turned the girl over.

'That was when José Luis told me to collect her clothes. The rest went off about 7 m from the car and began to dig a hole near a mezquite bush that was there.

'Because Charly had finished raping the girl, El Diablo went over to where the bundle of clothes was and got Charly out of the way and it was Charly who buried the bundle in the hole that they had made.

'When El Diablo finished raping the girl, he and Charly got the girl down on the front-seat passenger's side of the car and that was when El Diablo said, "Let's get it over with," and between the two of them they lifted her and went off with her into the darkness about 7 m almost in the direction where the clothes had been buried.

'Then José Luis and Gerardo went after them and I saw that the girl was moving her head like she was going to pass out and then I lost sight of them, so I went after them and could get close enough to see that Charlie (sic) and El Diablo had put her on the ground.

'Then José Luis bent down and gave her a slap and then gave her like five punches and at the same time he was squeezing her throat and the girl was moving like she was suffocating and making a noise like she needed air, until she stopped moving.

'Then all of us started to kick her all over her body, and then Gera, Charlie, and then El Diablo started to tear at her with their hands and then they dug a hole about 60 cm wide and deep, I do not remember, but the girl fitted into it exactly.

'Then we covered her up with soil and stamped the soil down with our feet, at the same time smoothing it over.

'Then we went back to the car and from there we drove back to the city centre. We went to the wine bar El Nacional, on the corner of Ugarte and Mariscal and, as I was getting out, José Luis said to me, "Do not say anything because if you do we will sort you out the way we have already told you we would."

'I recognise the girl I have told you about in a photograph of Rosario García Leal, from the Philips *maquiladora*.'

Rebels and devils. Rebels and a 'Devil', at least. The nicknames and slang and straggling syntax of the confessions all add to their power. To their ring of truth. But are they true? No one knows. That *Los Rebeldes* were a gang of young criminals seems reasonably certain, but there are many gangs of young criminals in Juárez, and in México, and in the world. And some of these gangs do indeed rape and abuse women. But few of them, surely, then make a habit of strangling and burying their victims, all of this done for money paid by a convicted rapist already behind bars.

And the members of the gang have accused the police of torturing confessions out of them, and shown the marks of it. Their lawyers have also pointed out that there is little evidence against them. True, but what there is, the prosecutors retort, is very strong. One of the gang was confronted with it by a presenter from ABC, the American Broadcasting Company, during 'Silent Screams in Juárez', a *20-20* special on the Juárez murders:

John Quinones [voice-over]: Two and a half years ago, authorities rounded up what they thought was a gang of serial killers known as 'Los Rebeldes', led by this man who called himself 'El Diablo'. Police say the gang tortured seventeen women, brutally assaulting them on this concrete slab before murdering them. Several of the girls had bite marks all over their bodies. We visited El Diablo in a Juárez prison and showed him a picture of one of his alleged victims. [On camera] Do you recognise this woman? *¿La conoces?* The police say you killed her. You raped her, tortured her.

Sergio Armendáriz, 'El Diablo': No.

John Quinones: No? Investigators say your teeth perfectly match the bite marks that were on her breast.

Sergio Armendáriz [through translator]: Those famous bite marks. They do not match.

John Quinones: Those are not your teeth?

Sergio Armendáriz: No.

John Quinones [voice-over]: But back at her forensics lab, Dr Rodríguez, the medical examiner, says these

imprints, the bite marks, leave no doubt that it was 'El
Diablo' who tortured at least three of the victims.
Authorities say they're confident they will convict him in
those murders. But what's troubling to this community is
that even while 'El Diablo' has been in jail, more than
fifty other women have been raped and murdered.
(Transcript of 'Silent Screams in Juárez', ABC's
Wednesday, January 20, 1999 transmission of *20–20*)

But is this *prueba odontológica* – 'dental proof', as Spanish
puts it – unassailable evidence of Armendáriz's guilt? No, not
*unassailable* evidence. México has always been notorious for
official corruption, particularly in the police and judiciary,
and more sophisticated forensic science must sometimes have
meant nothing more than more sophisticated ways for
suspects to be framed. But even on the supposition – and it
seems, admittedly, a strong one – that 'El Diablo' did leave
teeth-marks on the bodies of young women while he was
raping them, this does not prove that he was working with a
gang. Still less does it prove that he or the gang were working
for Sharif Sharif, being paid by the corpse to help him
establish his innocence. The police, under pressure to stem a
blood-red tide of sex murders, may simply have decided that
one rapist would help them to seal the case against another.
Armendáriz was arrested with his confederates, the story of
Sharif's machinations from behind bars invented, and acqui-
escence in it beaten into the gang.

For the simple fact remains that the arrest of *Los Rebeldes*
did not stem that blood-red tide: the murders stopped for a
time and then continued until *another* gang, also allegedly in
conspiracy with Sharif, were arrested. *Then* the tide reached a
high-water mark and seems, so far, to be lapping there, rising
no more. The questions, however, continue to flow. Would
the police have invented the story of a conspiracy between
Sharif and *Los Rebeldes* when it would so easily be undermined by the continuing murders? Perhaps, perhaps not.
Perhaps the police had picked up rumours of a conspiracy
between Sharif and an outside group, and thought, when they
arrested *Los Rebeldes*, that they had arrested this outside

group. When *Los Rebeldes* refused to confess, they were made to confess. If so, it would be a familiar story: the police, believing they have the guilty parties without the evidence necessary to secure a conviction, decide to invent the necessary evidence. Under this reading, *Los Rebeldes* are a kind of Mexican Guildford Four or Birmingham Six (famous cases in Britain of suspects convicted on fabricated or badly flawed evidence), and the police may have been just as shocked as the public when, with all members of the conspiracy apparently behind bars, the bodies of raped and mutilated young women began to turn up again on the desert outskirts and the building-lots of Juárez. Month after month after month after month.

Until the arrest of that other gang, *Los Choferes*. The Drivers.

## Thread

*Hilo m. Hebra larga y delgada que se forma retorciendo cualquier materia textil.*
Thread. Long, thin fibre produced by twisting some textile material.

'Behold, *when* we come into the land, thou shalt bind this line of scarlet thread in the window which thou didst let us down by . . .' (Book of Joshua, 2, xviii)

'Scarlet thread' is a Biblical phrase from the Book of Joshua, used to describe how a 'harlot' of Jericho and her family escape the otherwise indiscriminate massacre that follows the capture of the city by the Israelites:

And they utterly destroyed all that *was* in the city, both man and woman, young and old, and ox, and sheep, and ass, with the edge of the sword.

But Joshua said unto the two men that had spied out the country, 'Go into the harlot's house, and bring out thence the woman, and all that she hath . . .' (6, xxi–xxii)

'Scarlet thread' is used in a context of death in the Book of Joshua, and so translates smoothly and easily to a Book of Juárez. All serial killers may be said to weave a scarlet thread into the tapestry of life, and the moment they make a final, fatal mistake may be said to be the moment when the thread begins to unravel – when it is seized, tugged, begins to come loose and reveal the interconnections and hidden patterns of the crimes.

But the crimes of Juárez seem to have revealed not one scarlet thread but at least two, perhaps three: the thread woven by Sharif himself; the thread perhaps woven by a gang of Sharif's hirelings, the young psychopaths of a street-gang called *Los Rebeldes*; and the thread far more certainly woven by another group of Sharif's hirelings, the older men of an unofficial gang christened by the media *Los Choferes*, The Drivers. The moment when the last of these threads began to unravel was perhaps late on 13 March 1999 – a Saturday – when:

> A fourteen-year-old female employee of the Motores Eléctricos maquila was found barely alive on a ranch near the Pemex plant in the southwest part of Cd. Juárez. The assassin fortunately did not complete his crime, leaving the young girl for dead.
>
> Nancy, as she is known, had been severely beaten, raped and strangled; however when she lost consciousness the alleged perpetrator, Jesús Manuel Guardado Márquez, 26, a maquila bus driver, assumed she was dead and abandoned her. (*Frontera NorteSur*, April, 1999)

Guardado had a *nombre de apodo* – a nickname. Two of them, in fact. *El Tolteca*, The Toltec, and *El Dracula*, Dracula. After his arrest, which came about when, in hiding, he beat up his pregnant wife and was reported to the police by his sister, his confession led the authorities to other men and other nicknames: Augustín Toribio Castillo, José Gaspar Ceballos Chavez, Victor Moreno Rivera, Bernardo Hernando Fernández – 'El Kiani', 'El Gaspy', 'El Narco', 'El Samber' – Kiani, Gaspi, Druggie, St Bernard. Another act was about to open in the Comedy of Terrors created by Sharif in Ciudad Juárez, though, as I have suggested before, not all the players in the rest of the play were necessarily recruited from México.

# 7. Sinergia

## Sharks

*Tiburón m. Nombre dado a los peces selacios de cuerpo fusiforme y aletas pectorales grandes cuya boca, en la parte inferior de la cabeza, tiene forma de media luna y está provista de varias filas de dientes cortantes.*

Shark. Name given to selachian fish with streamlined bodies and large pectoral fins whose mouths, in the lower part of the head, are half-moon-shaped and filled with rows of cutting teeth.

About ten years ago, a survey was conducted to establish which word had the greatest impact on the greatest number of people. Researchers tested words like 'rape', 'death', 'murder', 'sex', 'love', 'snake', 'poison'. To their surprise, it was the word 'shark' which aroused the public's emotions more than any of the others. (*Great Shark Stories*, Valerie and Ron Taylor, 1978)

Blood in the water. In the open sea it can be a death knell, drawing sharks from great distances to participate in an uncouth, thrashing circle-dance centred on the writhing body of the victim – a feeding frenzy.

Translate this into the world of human beings, retaining one of the terms: blood. Blood on the streets. In the free media it can be a dinner-bell of income, drawing journalists from great distances to participate in an unseemly, squabbling circle-dance centred on the contorted body of the victim. Or the bodies of the victims. Particularly if the victim or victims are female.

This is what has happened in Juárez. Female blood was spilt on the streets there, and in the dust of the surrounding desert. The scent of it travelled very far, wafting south through Chihuahua state to México City and continental Latin America, north across the border to the United States and Canada, west and south across the Pacific to Australia, New Zealand and Japan, east across the Atlantic to Europe and the United Kingdom.

The following appears courtesy of the 9 September 1999 online edition of the BBC news:

Mexico's murder town. Bodies of young girls keep turning up. Tom Carver reports from a town on the

Mexico–US border where the murder rate of young women is horrifically high . . . 'It was around the beginning of 1995 that the police belatedly realised that a serial killer was haunting the unlit squatter camps like Anapra that ring Juárez. The bodies of young girls kept turning up.'

But were these journalists and their tape-recorders and camera lenses all that the scent of fresh female blood brought to Juárez? For consider that journalists do not work to feed merely their own appetites for death and pain, but also the appetites of their audience. All those millions watching, listening, and reading in the United States, being told of baffled police unable to protect the young and vulnerable women of a city just across the border in México. Blood in the water. Blood in the media. Victims to be had for the taking. Would it be surprising if one or more serial-killers certainly at work in the deep south of the United States pricked up their ears and wanted to learn more? If one or more of them dug out an interstate map and idly calculated how long it would take to drive to El Paso, Texas, and the border crossing to Juárez? If one or more of them decided that it was time to take a short vacation down Mexico way?

## Synergy

Synergy n. The working together of two or more drugs, muscles, etc., to produce an effect greater than the sum of their individual effects.

Jesus and Elvis are, it is said, the only human beings well enough known to everyone to be referred to by just their first names. *Aficionados* of true crime cannot quite match this with individuals, perhaps, but they can with couples. Two couples so far. Ian and Myra. Fred and Rose.

Perhaps a third couple began to be added to this infernal pantheon of anti-heroes when a bleeding woman, wearing only a 'padlocked metal collar', stumbled from a mobile home in Elephant Butte, New Mexico, with a tale of three days of enforced sexual torture and bondage. Ian and Myra. Fred and Rose. David and Cindy?

In the future perhaps, but today they must be identified by their full names: David Parker Ray and Cynthia 'Cindy' Lea Hendy. Ray stares out from his police identification photo like an ageing school caretaker, with no hint of his depraved tastes in eyes lined and pouched by the passage of fifty-nine years of hitherto unremarked life. Hendy, if anything, seems even more ordinary: blonde, plump, a thirty-nine-year-old woman who seems about to slide unprotesting into middle-age, and long, slow, comfortable years of retirement: TV, conversation, European holidays, grandchildren.

The testimony of their victim – and the two others who have come forward so far – contradicts all that more than a little. More than a lot. The naked woman who escaped in the padlocked collar told the police of three days of torture during which Ray chained her to a bed and molested her with 'sexual devices', attached wires to her breasts and passed agonising jolts of electricity through her body, and bound and suspended her from the ceiling of the mobile home while he whipped her with a 'leather object'. Hendy, meanwhile, stood guard cradling a revolver and threatening to shoot the victim if she tried to escape.

Having charged Ray with 'kidnap and criminal sexual penetration' and Hendy with 'kidnap and accessory to criminal sexual penetration', the police searched the makeshift torture chamber and emerged with a smorgasbord of sexual psychopathology.

Anatomy books, medical books 'and a chart depicting what appears to be methods of sexual torture and bondage' that were reportedly found in the trailer known as the toy box, along with 'photographs depicting women in various stages of bondage', a large coffinlike box and a diorama in a glass and wood case that contains 'dolls posed and painted in different positions depicting bondage and sexual sadism'. One affidavit said the coffinlike box was about seven feet long and had carpeting inside. It also had ventilation holes, 'so that a person could be secured in the box and at the same time kept alive for an extended period of time.' (*Albuquerque Tribune*)

More disturbing even than these, however, were maps of the nearby Elephant Butte Lake with 'X's marking various points along the shoreline and on the island of Kettle Top, and about one hundred videotapes. The last, of course, raises immediate echoes of a duo from a side-gallery of the Sex Criminal Hall of Fame: the American 'Vietnam veteran' Leonard Lake and, from Hong Kong, his 'accomplice' Charles Ng, who together abducted three women and kept them as their 'sex slaves' in a specially built torture chamber beneath their cabin near Wisleyville, in Calaveras County, California. The three women were murdered when their captors finally tired of them, as were the two young children abducted with their 'sex slave' mothers. (See *The Serial Killers: a study in the psychology of violence*, Colin Wilson and Donald Seaman, Virgin Publishing, London, 1990.)

As also proved true of Parker and Hendy, Lake and Ng had videotaped their torture of the women, informing one that she would 'wash for us, clean for us, fuck for us'. Lake's fantasy, revealed in a journal discovered surrounded by chains and hooks in the torture chamber, was that of a 'woman who does exactly what she is told to do and nothing else. There is no sexual problem with a submissive woman. There are no frustrations – only pleasure and contentment.' (*Ibid.*, ch. 7.)

An audio-tape discovered in Ray's mobile home has revealed the same turn of mind in this other couple. Used in the 'indoctrination' of his victims, it informed them that they were 'going to be kept naked and chained up like an animal and used and abused any way we want to' (*Albuquerque Tribune*). The voice, positively identified as Ray's by the New Mexico State Police investigator John Briscoe, then goes on to talk of using Phenobarbital and sodium pentothal on women 'to erase memories and make them susceptible to hypnosis'. There are echoes here of Jeffrey Dahmer, the 'Milwaukee Cannibal' who experimented with trepanning and injections of bleach into the brains of his victims in an attempt to create a perfectly obedient sex-zombie.

Homosexual Dahmer, however, operated alone: Ray seems to have operated not merely as half of a heterosexual couple but also, like Frederick West, as a kind of godfather of rape, sexual torture, and, it is believed, serial murder: his thirty-two-year-old daughter Glenda 'Jesse' Ray and a twenty-seven-year-old acquaintance, Dennis Roy Yancy, have been charged alongside him and Hendy; Ray *fille* with participation of her father in twelve separate counts of kidnap, sexual torture, and conspiracy; and Yancy with the murder of a twenty-two-year-old woman called Marie B. Parker, who had disappeared without trace from an Elephant Butte bar in 1997.

The investigation of Ray's activities, still in its early days, seems to be following a familiar trajectory: the fortuitous and highly fortunate escape of an intended victim; the arrest of the accused and the issuing of firm denials of wrongdoing from his quickly hired defence lawyer; the searching of the home of the accused and discovery of items suspicious in themselves and offering clues to the truly damning evidence: the graves of 'as many as fourteen people'. The police are now searching for these in the 'arroyos' – the beds, sometimes seasonally dry, of a river or stream – of Sierra County, calling upon the assistance of 'ground-penetrating radar and cadaver-sniffing dogs'.

Those familiar with the Moors Murders or the 'House of Death' at Cromwell Street, Gloucester, could provide parallels for each of the steps taken by the investigation so far, and it seems perfectly possible that 'David and Cindy' will, very early in the third millennium, join 'Ian and Myra' and 'Fred and Rose' as instantly recognisable icons of twentieth-century sex-murder. Already forensic psychologists are finding patterns in what is known so far of Ray's behaviour that point to his fitting the profile of a typical serial killer. One characteristic of the serial killer is that he will wish to revisit the graves of his victims, reliving the excitement of the crimes and feeding a ghoulish delight with a secret knowledge that only he and his accomplices possess. Ian Brady and Myra Hindley did this both literally and photographically, when Brady photographed a smiling Hindley hugging a puppy atop a child's grave dug into the turf of the bleak moors that overlook Manchester. So far Ray seems to have done it only literally: as already mentioned, an 'X' on one of the maps discovered by the police in his mobile home marks an island called Kettle Top in Elephant Butte Lake. From the windows of his mobile home, Ray only had to raise his eyes to see this island.

Even more characteristic of the serial killer is, however, a penchant for the keeping of souvenirs of the victim:

> FBI profilers believe Ray, 59, kept items from the victims, including jewellery, hair or fingernails . . . The profilers say people who commit serial crimes collect such trinkets and keep them in a cache so they can relive the experiences. (DA: HENDY SAID RAY KILLED UP TO 14, *Albuquerque Tribune*)

Is it here that the crimes in Elephant Butte, New Mexico, intermesh with the crimes in Ciudad Juárez, Chihuahua? Suly Ponce, the head of the Special Investigator's Tribunal in Juárez, has drawn the media's attention to a strange feature of some of the murders discovered there so far. She has remarked of some of the victims that:

> 'They had no panties. None. They could have all their other clothes – shoes, socks, stockings, bra. But no underpants.' (THE DEATHS THAT HAUNT JUÁREZ, Mary Beth Sheridan, *Los Angeles Times*)

It seemed that a serial killer in Juárez had been collecting souvenirs of his crimes, and that he, like Ray, had a fetish about female hair:

> Victims [in Juárez] were in their teens or early 20s, slim and petite, almost always with long dark hair. (SIX NEW SLAYINGS REVEAL THAT KILLER IS STILL ON THE LOOSE, Mark Smith, *Houston Chronicle*, 1996)

But could this collector of sex-souvenirs and trichophile – hair-fetishist – in México be the same collector of sex-souvenirs and trichophile as in New Mexico? In short, could David Parker Ray have been responsible for some of the crimes in Juárez?

On geographical grounds alone, the answer must be yes. Nowhere in New Mexico is very far from Texas or the Mexican border, but Ray committed his crimes, and is said to have buried his victims, in Sierra County, in eastern New Mexico, almost on the state boundary with Texas. This put him – and Hendy – within very easy striking distance of El Paso and the crossing to Juárez: a couple of hours' comfortable driving there, a couple of hours' comfortable driving back.

And hair-fetishism and the collection of sex-souvenirs are by no means the only darkly disturbing echoes to reverberate between the accounts of the crimes in Elephant Butte and Juárez. One of the women to survive Ray's attentions, tracked down by the police through a 'distinctive swan tattoo on her right leg' that was visible on one of the videos found in Ray's home, has testified that:

'I remember him telling me he was into a satanic group. He said members of the group had been watching me and they wanted me as a sex toy.' (DA: HENDY SAID RAY KILLED UP TO 14, *Albuquerque Tribune*)

There are two echoes of the crimes in Juárez here. The first is the tattoo that allowed Ray's victim to be identified. One of those accused of the crimes in Juárez was similarly identified by a tattoo:

His identifying characteristics were confirmed by the picture released by the authorities [in Chihuahua], such as two tattoos on his arms, a rose and hands joined in prayer with an inscription that reads 'My Mother Carmen'. (*El Diario de Juárez*)

And what is the second darkly disturbing echo raised by the testimony of the swan-tattooed victim from the account of the crimes in *El Diario de Juárez*? It is this:

The motive of the crimes continues to be unclear, but various theories suggest that they are connected with a traffic in human organs, the white-slave trade, or . . .

Or '*ritos satánicas*'. Satanic rites.

# 8. Satan

*Satanás o Satán, jefe de los demonios, espíritu del mal.*
Satanas or Satan, chief of demons, spirit of evil.

ἐθεώρουν τὸν Σατανᾶν ὡς ἀστραπὴν ἐκ τοῦ οὐρανοῦ πεσόντα. 'I beheld
Satan as lightning fall from the heaven.' (The Gospel of St Luke, x, 18)

Satanism. The worship of Satan, 'chief of demons, spirit of
evil'. And arch-rebel. In México, a nation forged by rebellion,
that makes him a figure of special, particular power. To swear
allegiance to Satan is to swear allegiance to the first and
greatest of rebels, and to join in a rebellion against the Lord
of the Universe. And, of course, in a rebellion against His
earthly representatives: the Roman Catholic Church.

For if the true piquancy and *frisson* of Satanism is only
possible in a society heavily influenced by some form of
Christianity, the expression of Satanism is always conditioned
by its origins in Roman Catholicism. The United States, for
example, is a Protestant nation, and yet the symbol of
Satanism there, as in Roman Catholic México, is the inverted
crucifix, despite the fact that the crucifix is not something
upon which Protestantism has ever chosen to place much
emphasis.

For Protestantism, another rebellion against the Roman
Catholic Church, rebelled by negation and extirpation; Satanism rebelled by *inversion*. Compare two cases: Protestant and
Satanic attacks on a Christian church. During the English
Civil War of the seventeenth century and the Commonwealth
that followed it, extreme Protestants raided churches in search
of the symbols of Roman Catholicism. Where and when they
found such symbols, they destroyed them, smashing statues
with hammers and axes, whitewashing religious paintings,
tearing out rood-screens and altar-rails. Their strategy was
*iconoclasm* – literally, the breaking of icons.

The strategy of Satanism might therefore be described as
*iconomachy*, literally a war with icons. But that 'war with' bears

two senses: it is a war against, and a war by means of. Satanists do not usually destroy the 'icons' of a Christian church: the crucifixes, the altar and its paraphernalia, the hymn books and missals. Instead, they corrupt them, co-opt them to an opposite end. In short, they *invert* them. Satanism is Roman Catholicism inverted – Roman Catholicism in negative. The Holy wafer is at the heart of ritual in both religions, but where Roman Catholicism honours and elevates it, Satanism degrades and defiles it. Where the Roman Catholic mass is a preserve of patriarchiality, the Satanic mass is served upon the naked body of a woman in whose vagina the Holy wafer will be inserted for commingling with the semen of the celebrant Satanic priest, who tradition holds must also be a defrocked Roman Catholic priest. Where the sacred blood of the Roman Catholic mass is subtilised into symbolic wine and partaken of in reverent sips, the sacred blood of the Satanic mass is literal blood, partaken of in greedy gulps from a chalice held beneath the slashed throat of a child. Or of a virgin, a young woman with an unbroken hymen between her thighs. For where Roman Catholicism celebrates the *life* of a virgin – the Virgin Mary – to the point (for Protestants, beyond the point) at which she threatens to overshadow her son Jesus Christ, Satanism celebrates the *death* of a virgin. In short, where there is white in Roman Catholicism, there is black in Satanism; where there is black in Roman Catholicism, there is white in Satanism. All this is concentrated and distilled in those two Satanic symbols: the *crux inverta*, the inverted crucifix, and the *virgo immolata*, the sacrificed virgin.

These facts of history and psycho-culture underlie and resonate within the claims that '*ritos satánicos*' are involved in the Juárez murders. Young women, many of them literal virgins, are kidnapped, raped, and tortured, treated with extreme violence and contumely, before being strangled or stabbed to death and *buried*. In this last fact we find another echo of anti-Christian ritual, for the inhabitants of pagan Latin America, like those of old pagan Europe, would consecrate and protect buildings by the sacrifice of human beings whose corpses were then buried in the foundations.

As time went on, this sacrificial ritual (in the same progression that saw the literal blood-drinking that underlies the Eucharist transmuted into symbolic wine-drinking) was undertaken with animals instead. Perhaps in Juárez we have seen a return to the older, purer ritual, for much of outlying Juárez is occupied by building lots, ideal for the burial of murder-victims whose graves will soon be covered by cement and steel. But can we extrapolate from this to the existence of some Satan-worshipping building contractor, hiring men to protect his investments by the murder and burial of young women beneath the foundations?

Such an extrapolation seems doubtful, even (perhaps certainly) ridiculous, but there is no need to make it, for there are easier alternatives. We could suppose the existence of an allegorical spirit of ancient evil brooding above the psychogeographic landscape of Juárez, nourished by the pain and misery of its inhabitants and sliding tendrils into the receptive unconsciousness of men like Sharif and 'El Tolteca'. The tendrils bloom into the consciousness of these men with ideas: the idea of the rape and murder of young women, the idea of their burial in the harsh sand of empty or half-constructed building lots.

For parallel ideas do not necessarily indicate a common origin. Instead, they can indicate common conditions. Iron heated and pounded behaves similarly everywhere in the world; minds wounded and twisted produce similar psychopathologies everywhere in the world. Rape and murder have been found in every culture and at every time, and their expression in ritualistic form may presuppose only particular, unconnected corruptions of a general human nature, not an underlying network of shared history and tradition. The ritual of 'foundation burial' may have arisen spontaneously and independently many times around the world, and may re-arise spontaneously and independently wherever the conditions are right. In Juárez the conditions may have been right: the sexually provoking presence of young women, the ready availability of burial space.

Perhaps we could read into the ritual an even deeper significance, stretching beyond even the most general human nature into our evolutionary past: many carnivorous animals bury uneaten portions of their slaughtered prey as a precaution against scavengers and to avoid alarming still-living members of the prey species. Perhaps Sharif and his confederates have resurrected this ancient instinct, dredging it up from the ancient centres of the brain devoted to the most basic patterns of behaviour: sex and feeding.

This would explain too the bite-marks found on the bodies of some of the victims. Like re-triggerable fragments of outmoded code buried in a computer program, ancient instincts are buried in the human brain, quiescent – *repressed* – under normal conditions, but always ready to be re-triggered by psychosis and induce the anomalous behaviour of an attack by biting from a creature whose teeth are no longer suitable for it. It is difficult and inefficient for a human being to inflict life-threatening injuries on another human being by biting, and the appearance of this behaviour amongst some rapists seems to represent a psychological atavism: the re-emergence of an ancestor's behaviour in a modern descendant.

The rituals of Satanism could be viewed as a deliberate, conscious attempt to re-awaken these ancestral instincts, to provoke the omophagy – the eating of raw flesh – that was seen in the ancient rites of Dionysus and Bacchus. The Satanic mass is a kind of inverted behavioural therapy of deconditioning that uses the drinking of fresh human blood to accustom its participants to the breaking of the ultimate dietary taboo: cannibalism. And yet the drinking of blood is, for some, an end in itself: the beverage of choice for such archangels of the Satanic hierarchy as the vampire-king Count Dracula.

The Transylvanian legend of Dracula was taken up, adapted, and transmitted to the rest of the world by the Irish novelist Bram Stoker (1847–1912), and it and its connotations are as well known in México as anywhere else. So it was that Spanish-speaking readers of the Juárez newspaper reports of the arrest of a gang of bus-drivers for rape and murder would not have been puzzled by the nickname attached to one of them. Guardado Márquez is known both as 'El Tolteca' – the Toltec – and as 'El Dracula'. In Spanish the vowels and consonants of the latter have appropriately pure, mono-phthongal European values: draa-koo-laa. The first two syllables, in fact, raise an echo from an ancient European text: 'Et ecce draco magnus rufus'. This is the Latin of what was once the only lawful form of the Bible in Catholic Europe, and can be rendered in English like this: 'And behold a great red dragon'. (The Revelation of St John the Divine, xii, 3.)

Dracula: draco. Dracula: dragon. And the dragon is, of course, a Biblical symbol of Satan, found both in the New Testament and in the Old. Dracula is a dragon, and dragons are famed in such hagiographies as that of St George for their propensity to demand virgin sacrifice. Guardado Márquez, 'El Dracula', was an ancient word made modern flesh, a dragon sacrificing virgins to himself and his own pursuit of pleasure.

How did Márquez acquire his apodo vampírico, his vampiric nickname? Newspaper reports do not tell us, but perhaps there was a sense of something sinister about him, a whiff of a particular evil that was redolent of the legend of the vampire-king and his atavistically long and pointed canine teeth. And the men who christened Márquez with this sobriquet must have already been attuned to its anti-Christian, Satanic resonances, for they live in a city named for an anti-Christian rebel:

> Santa Anna was overthrown in 1855 by Benito Juárez, whose liberal reforms included many anti-clerical measures . . . In 1862, Miramon [a former president of México] appealed to Empress Eugénie, consort of Napoleon III, saying that steps must be taken against Juárez and his anti-Christian policies. (The Hutchinson Softback Encyclopedia)

This French intervention brought about another war and another victory for Juárez, sealing his status as a folk-hero and encouraging, perhaps, the choice of a border city for his onomastic memorial. Ciudad Juárez, facing the United States across the Río Bravo, bears in its name a defiant challenge: the name of the rebel who faced down foreign interference and intervention directed from Paris, the Vatican City, and Washington.

With unconscious irony the outside world, seeing México through American eyes, refers to 'Juárez' as just that, unaware that it is confusing a city with a man. In México, Juárez must be Ciudad Juárez, Juárez City, for Mexicans, in another piece of unconscious irony, are respectful of their rebel-heroes, even adoring of them. Their chief political party, winner of an unbroken string of national elections, is the *Partido Revolucionario Institucional*: the Institutional Revolutionary Party. Perhaps this oxymoron can be seen as a symbol of México's endemic corruption. The concepts of revolution and rebellion have become simply another tool by which the powerful exploit the masses for their own enrichment and pleasure, and the ring of names like Juárez, a folk-hero of México's historic quest for freedom, acquires a flat, sour note in popular Mexican discourse.

This corruption of rebellion would fit well with the legend of Satan, whose defiance of God was inspired by the lust for personal advance: 'To reign is worth ambition, though in hell:/Better to reign in hell, than serve in heav'n'. (*Paradise Lost*, Milton, lines 260–1.) To institutionalise revolution, as México has done, and to commemorate rebels and revolutionaries in the names of your cities is to contradict the very concept one wishes to honour, and the message received by the youth of México can only be a distorted one: rebellion is not for the good of others but for the good of oneself, not to overturn power alone, but to overturn power in order to become powerful oneself.

The message spoken by the final two syllables of 'Ciudad Juárez' across the Río Bravo then becomes not a defiant challenge but a sardonic chuckle. And the first to hear this chuckle will be, of course, the inhabitants of El Paso, Texas. Perhaps this helps to explain a man who is probably the most famous son of the Texan city:

One of the most recent of these so-called 'high-scoring' serial killers was Richard Ramirez, alias 'The Night Stalker' – twenty-eight years of age, unmarried, a drifter and satanist [*sic*] from El Paso, Texas. In the fifteen months between June 1984 and August 1985 the Night

Stalker murdered thirteen people and sexually assaulted
several others in the suburbs of Los Angeles . . . Men
were shot or stabbed as they slept. The women were
beaten, raped and sexually abused, regardless of age:
most were murdered by strangulation, stabbing or
shooting. Their children (of both sexes, some as young as
six) were either sexually assaulted in their homes, or
abducted, to be raped and sodomised before being
turned loose on the streets, miles away. All Ramirez'
attacks were marked by extreme cruelty; on one occasion
he gouged a woman's eyes out. He 'signed' some of his
murders by sketching in lipstick a pentagram – a
five-pointed star, often associated with satanism – at the
scene of the crime, either on the victim's body or the wall
above. (*The Serial Killers: a study in the psychology of
violence*, Colin Wilson and Donald Seaman, Virgin
Publishing, 1990)

There is an immediate echo here of Victor Moreno Rivera,
'El Narco', the Druggie, a member of *Los Choferes*, the bus
drivers who the Mexican authorities said have been paid by
Sharif to rape and murder in his stead:

The first to speak with reporters was Victor Moreno
Rivera. The American citizen, twenty-eight years old,
[said] that he had been imprisoned in Doña Ana county
for smuggling marijuana into the United States and for
robbery, which was why he decided to settle after nearly
a year in Ciudad Juárez.
    'I came to work here so I did not have to pay a
monthly fine of forty dollars, and I began to work
cleaning cars. A little later I went to work selling cars that
I brought from El Paso, and that is what I have been
doing for the past six months.' (*El Diario de Juárez*)

Like Richard Ramirez, 'El Narco' was twenty-eight years old
on his arrest, a Latino American citizen, familiar with El Paso,
and accused of rape and murder. He is accused of being
Sharif's contact with the outside world, travelling regularly to

the *CeReSo* to hand over evidence of the crimes and receive envelopes of money to be handed out to the remainder of *Los Choferes*, the Bus Drivers.

# 9. Slice

*Cortar v.t. Separar por medio de un instrumento cortante.*
Slice. Transitive verb. Separate by means of a cutting instrument.

An electron microscope can reveal the tiniest details of structure in a plant or animal cell – with one great disadvantage. The cell can no longer be living when it does so. It must be treated, prepared, bathed in toxic chemicals, and the stream of radiation with which the electron microscope plucks its secrets from it would kill it anyway. Scientists can see in exceedingly fine detail what a cell looks like, but not how it works. They see a snapshot, not a film.

Murder is like an electron microscope – revealing the tiniest details of life – but murder offers more than a snapshot. The investigations that take place after a murder can cover days of the victim's life, preserving details that would otherwise be lost among the forgotten debris of history. Who, for example, would have bothered to record the day-to-day lives of prostitutes in a working-class district of nineteenth-century London? Who, that is, if those prostitutes had not been victims of Jack the Ripper?

No one, it seems likely, but those prostitutes *were* the victims of Jack the Ripper, and their day-to-day lives *were* recorded. Similarly, who would be bothering to record the lives of the *maquiladora* workers and bar-girls of Juárez if they were not falling victim to a serial killer or serial killers? Again, no one, it seems very likely. But those *maquiladora* workers and bar-girls are falling victim to murder, and their lives are being recorded. Sometimes after their deaths. At autopsy:

Case 16, 30 July [1996] – Rocío Miranda Aguero: Rocío Miranda Aguero, 28 years old, manageress of the nightclub Top Capos, was found by children in a 200-litre drum full of corrosive acid, with only her hands and feet remaining undissolved. She was identified by

her silicone [breast-] implants. She had been abducted
by 17 people. In the same house there were a female
servant and a two-month-old baby, the daughter of the
murdered woman, both of whom were miraculously
saved by hiding. [This is taken from the ParaSagrario
website, as are the other 'case study' quotations which
follow.]

There, in seventy-three words of terse, sinewy forensic
Spanish, is a slice of Juárez life, paradoxically fixed and
preserved and magnified by an act of enforced death. The
report is like a prose-poem, its phrases almost as corrosive on
the emotions and sensibilities of the reader as the acid Rocío
Aguero was submerged in and devoured by.

And more, much more, can be inferred than is explicitly
stated. The 'silicone implants' that enabled the identification
of Aguero's otherwise almost entirely dissolved corpse suggest
a strong American influence on Juárez – an influence easily
confirmed by reference to foreign tourist guides for the city:

When visiting Ciudad Juárez, bear in mind that it has the
highest consumer price index in México . . . Many
everyday consumer items are US Goods brought in from
El Paso. In spite of the relatively high cost of living, the
city has México's fifth highest US expatriate population –
more than 28,000 at last count. (*Northern Mexico
Handbook*, Joe Cummings, Moon Publications, 1998)

It is another piece of circumstantial evidence for the
involvement of a home-based American citizen in the Juárez
murders. In another Mexican city or town, further south
perhaps, more inaccessible, an American might stand out, be
noted and remembered by bar tenders or hotel workers, street
vendors or school children whom the police could then
question and obtain a description from. In Juárez there are too
many Americans for this to happen. An American serial killer
could come and go as he pleased in the reasonable confidence
that he would not stand out even if memories were jogged by
a *direct* link with the death of a woman. Examine another slice

of Juárez life paradoxically fixed and magnified by the act of murder:

> Case 25, 21 September [1998] – A woman has her throat cut with a knife in the Juárez Hotel. She was Dutch [according to] documents found in a pillowcase and was found under the bed stripped naked. It is calculated that she had been dead 14 hours. The room had been rented by a man of North American appearance who has not yet been traced.

Note that phrase: 'a man of North American appearance'. Citizens of the United States are recognisable as such in México, but in a city like Juárez, home to a large expatriate American community and visited by many American tourists, recognising someone's nationality on sight is not the same as remembering that someone clearly when he or she is out of sight.

So who was that 'man of North American appearance'? A first-time, one-off murderer, brought to the crime in a fit of rage or drunkenness, fleeing the scene in remorse and horror? The nature of the woman's death would suggest otherwise: slitting a woman's throat is not the usual means adopted by a first-time murderer. It suggests a familiarity with extreme violence, bespeaks someone ready to engage in what the Spanish calls '*guerra a cuchillo*': war to the knife.

The nakedness of the murdered woman and her nationality are also suggestive of more than a one-off murder. Nakedness implies sex, and sex and death imply some form of psychopathology in the killer. And the woman's nationality? It implies that she was almost certainly a stranger to Juárez herself, very likely a newcomer, with no close friends or relatives to press the police for a solution to her murder. If one were an American serial killer looking for a victim in Juárez, a Dutchwoman, citizen of a small country thousands of kilometres away, would be almost perfect, particularly at that stage of the wider killings. By 21 September 1998, Mexican women would have been becoming less and less accessible to serial killers. Even young and naïve *maquiladora* workers from the south, now far from family and friends, had feminists and political activists working hard on their behalf, forcing the state authorities and *maquiladora* companies to take measures for their employees' safety:

Factories have started issuing pepper spray to female employees. The government has done sweeps to find underage employees like the young survivor ['Nancy']. It has also demanded that bus drivers be tested for drugs.
(THE DEATHS THAT HAUNT JUAREZ, Mary Beth Sheridan, *Los Angeles Times*)

And consider that the previous murders must have operated a kind of natural selection amongst the young women of Juárez, eliminating the easiest targets, the most foolish and reckless, the most desperate of those who conformed to what seems to have been the killers' ideal victim profile: young, slender, *guapa* (attractive), and with long, dark hair.

Foreign women very rarely turn up in the list of victims compiled by the ParaSagrario Consortium, and perhaps the Dutchwoman – still unnamed – represented the first of what would have been an increasing trend, the target of a putative American serial killer who had crossed to kill in this Satanic playground of death: Juárez, the rebels' city named after a rebel in a country of institutionalised rebellion.

But at the time of writing, the serial rape and murder of young women in Juárez seems to have stopped. *Los Choferes* are behind bars and the abused and mutilated bodies, or the skeletal remains of abused and mutilated bodies, are no longer turning up in the empty building lots of Juárez or in the surrounding desert. But does this prove that the serial killers responsible are all behind bars? No, it merely *suggests* it. But, as I have stressed elsewhere, serial killing is a 'profession' that places a premium on intelligence and cunning, and one or more of the serial killers responsible may have decided to transfer his attentions to the women of some other city in some other region.

# 10. Charisma

*Carisma m. Don espiritual otorgado a grupos o individuos. Fascinación, gran prestigio del que gozan algunas personas.*

Charisma. Spiritual gift granted to groups or individuals. Fascination, special power possessed by some people.

In his posthumous book *Vom Kriege* (1833) – *On War* – the Prussian general Karl von Clausewitz (1780–1831) outlined the four types of officer and their respective values to a commander. The best kind of officer was, he said, one who was intelligent, but lazy. He will obey orders efficiently, and act on his own initiative when necessary, but not otherwise. After him came the stupid and lazy officer, who will obey orders and never try to act on his own initiative. After him came the intelligent and industrious officer, who will try to improve on the orders he is given, and will act on his own initiative whenever he can. Last of all came the stupid and industrious officer, who is disastrous in all ways.

Apply this reasoning to the serial killer. Suppose we take the concept of 'best' here to mean 'best for society'. The best kind of serial killer would be, then, the stupid and lazy one. He is likely to be caught after his first crime, without having had the chance to kill again (and so, of course, will never become a recognised serial killer). After him comes the stupid but industrious serial killer. He will be caught easily, but may have had time to commit several murders during the time the police are hunting for him. After him comes the intelligent but lazy serial killer. He will kill for a long time, and may never be caught, but being lazy will not kill very many. Last and worst of all – for society – comes the intelligent and industrious serial killer. He too will kill for a long time and he too may never be caught, but whether he is caught or not, he will kill very many.

Sharif was the last kind of serial killer: intelligent and industrious. His were the best of crimes, and the worst of crimes. The best for the sex-criminal *manqués* who cheer men such as him on from the sidelines, the worst from the point of view of society. No one knows how many women Sharif has killed in Juárez, and no one knows whether Sharif killed only in Juárez, and only in Juárez after he emigrated to work there for a *maquiladora*. After the first two of the rapes he committed in Florida and Texas, he should have been an automatic candidate for deportation from the United States as an undesirable alien.

But Sharif committed two rapes, then went on to commit more, and the United States Immigration Service only undertook proceedings against him in 1993, when he was employed by Benchmark Research and Technology of Midland, Texas. The deportation hearing took place in a city in the same state, a couple of hundred kilometres further east and nearer the Tex-Mex border. In fact, right *on* the Tex-Mex border.

Tim Madigan's article from the *Seattle Times*, 1999 entitled ' "Monster" Beats the System' said:

> 'The move to México had been Sharif's idea, Benchmark CEO Wayne Kinsey said in a recent interview. Sharif had become familiar with Ciudad Juárez during his deportation hearings in El Paso, just across the Rio Grande.'

Sharif was not imprisoned during the later stages of the hearing, and was at liberty to come and go as he pleased when his presence was not required in court. Accordingly, he must have come and gone in a way many inhabitants of El Paso do, back and forth across the Rio Grande, from El Paso to Juárez, back again from Juárez to El Paso. As one American tourist guide remarks of Juárez:

> 'For residents of neighboring El Paso it's a destination in its own right for food, nightlife, shopping, and greyhound and horse racing.' (*Northern Mexico Handbook*, Joe Cummings, Moon Publications, 1998)

Food, shopping, greyhound and horse racing. And night-life:

> There seemed a strange stillness over everything; but as I
> listened I heard as if from far down the valley the
> howling of many wolves. The Count's eyes gleamed, and
> he said, 'Listen to them – the children of the night. What
> music they make!' Seeing, I suppose, some expression in
> my face strange to him, he added, 'Ah, sir, you dwellers
> in the city cannot enter into the feelings of the hunter.'

That is chapter two of Bram Stoker's *Dracula* (1897), but the
Count is wrong. Some dwellers in the city *can* enter into the
feelings of the hunter, because some dwellers in the city are
also hunters. And they do not even need to leave the city to
hunt. Or want to leave it. For there can be a *música de la
noche*, a 'music of the night', in the city as well as deep in the
Transylvanian forests, though, like the moon-worshipping
song of wolves, it is a music whose beauty only a particular
kind of mind can appreciate:

> 'He demonstrated how two of them would grab the
> victim by the neck and strangle her between them, often
> until the vertebrae cracked,' Carmona said. He said, 'That
> made such a nice cracking sound.' (FORENSICS EXPERT
> STRUGGLES WITH WORK, Mark Stevenson, Associated Press)

The man who thought the cracking of female vertebrae
'made such a nice cracking sound' was Jesús Guardado
Márquez, El Tolteca, the leader of the bus drivers hired by
Sharif, whose own tastes in music remain veiled. Sharif
certainly, however, must have been exposed to yet another
'music of the night', for during his trips to Juárez from El Paso
and the deportation hearing there:

> Sharif would soon discover Ugarte Street, the seedy strip
> a few blocks from the mission square in the bustling
> downtown, the place in Juárez that was a sexual
> psychopath's dream.

On Ugarte and nearby streets, rough taverns like Joe's Place, Tuna Country, Casino Deportivo, and Noa-Noa's tumbled one unto another – lairs of the street gangs who ran the area's drug trade and prostitution. Hundreds of rickety buses rumbled onto Ugarte around the clock, depositing thousands of naïve teenage girls with painted nails and fresh lipstick. They were part of the legion of workers in foreign-owned factories, the *maquiladoras*, girls who made $3 a day, then stepped from their buses downtown and virtually onto the laps of men who bore them ill. ('MONSTER' BEATS THE SYSTEM, Tim Madigan, The *Seattle Times*, 1999)

As the egregious American heavy-metal band Guns'n'Roses once proclaimed: 'Welcome to the Jungle'. After his emigration to Juárez, Sharif became a predator of this jungle, a big cat, a jaguar, glossy-coated, sheathing razor-claws in velvet pads, supremely confident in his primacy and his ability to hunt down his prey by cunning and charisma:

On Ugarte, Sharif was taller than most. He spoke halting Spanish. And in a world of blue jeans and T-shirts, Sharif favored expensive watches and gaudy jewelry, silk shirts and turtlenecks, sports coats and dress shoes. (A MONSTER EXPOSED Tim Madigan with Juan Antonio Ramos, The *Fort Worth Star-Telegram*)

This sartorial elegance and regard for personal appearance will be familiar to readers of Anthony Burgess's *A Clockwork Orange* (1962), whose literally and onomastically lawless anti-hero, Alex, is also noticeable for his concern for appearance and cleanliness. Yet Anthony Burgess was not inventing the characteristics of his ultra-violent protagonist. A link between, on the one hand, a cat-like obsession with personal hygiene and grooming and, on the other, a propensity to extreme violence is found not only in the fictional Alex but also in real psychopaths and serial killers such as Dennis Nilsen, who is described in Brian Masters' *Killing for Company* as:

tall and slim, slightly stooped, with . . . thick brown hair.
He habitually wore dark trousers and a pale grey tweed
jacket, blue shirt, dark blue tie [and was] clean and tidy
. . . he wore rimless spectacles and was clean-shaven.

It was also found in Peter Sutcliffe, the Yorkshire Ripper:

All the same she [Carol Jones, an early girlfriend of
Sutcliffe's] was happy to be out with him, a smart, clean,
always tidy beau, who didn't swear and never showed
any sign of violence . . . [B]ecause the bathroom was to
one side of the house it was noticeable that when
Sutcliffe did get out of his old clothes to go out it took
him a long time to prepare himself; he would pay
particular attention to his hair. (*The Yorkshire Ripper: an
in-depth study of a mass killer and his methods*, Roger
Cross, HarperCollins)

As is described elsewhere, the attraction of women to men
is mediated by evidence of success. Serial killers, pop singers,
and athletes are all successful, and one way their success
manifests itself is in their prominence. They are noticed,
observed, talked about. Only the last of these might seem to
happen to serial killers before their arrest and imprisonment,
but that is in fact not necessarily so. Many serial killers are
prominent before their arrest and the attendant publicity. It is
merely that they are not identified as serial killers before their
arrest. The same underlying insecurities and abnormalities as
drive them to acts of rape and murder also often drive them
to positions of prominence in business and at work:

The management [of Clark's, a haulage company near
Bradford, northern England] had been so impressed with
Sutcliffe, regarding him as possessing all the virtues
required by the best lorry drivers, that he was chosen to
appear in a promotional brochure for the firm. He is
shown, hair in place, beard neatly trimmed as usual,
behind the wheel of 'Wee Willie' [his lorry], and a giant
enlargement of the photograph was given pride of place

in the entrance to the firm's offices. (*The Yorkshire Ripper: an in-depth study of a mass killer and his methods*, Roger Cross, HarperCollins, 1993)

But Sharif and Sutcliffe shared more than just this concern for their appearance and professional ability. Like Sharif, Sutcliffe had charisma, and a charisma that women found attractive. Susan Kelly, a typist and switchboard operator who was the only female working at Clark's while Sutcliffe drove a lorry for the firm, had, according to Roger Cross, 'always been struck by his pleasantness, his politeness, and particularly by the fact that she never heard him swear, something of a record among lorry drivers'.

This is echoed again by the Sharif case. During his trial for rape in Palm Beach, Florida, Sharif was represented by a defence lawyer called Greg Scott. Scott knew of the violence and sexual nature of his client's crimes, and yet found himself unable to resist his charisma.

Tim Madigan, again, from '"Monster" Beats the System' in the *Seattle Times*, 1999:

'But Scott also couldn't help being charmed by his client. Sharif was personable, funny and intelligent. He always treated Scott with respect. Criminal lawyers are used to dealing with the dregs of society. That in no way seemed to describe Sharif.'

And, in a sense, it was not the way to describe Sharif. Language and the instinctive systems of belief on which it is based mislead us in our relations with other human beings. 'Sharif' is a personal name, and we suppose that a personal name somehow attaches to a permanent entity: a body and mind that may change radically over time, but will do so slowly, in response to plainly visible influences from their environment. Similarly, we suppose that changes in a body and mind taking place over short periods of time will be related by simple steps to some factor in the environment.

It is suspected, for example, that Sharif had been raping and murdering women long before he emigrated to México, and one former acquaintance called John Pascoe has told of how he met a young girl in Sharif's apartment in New Hope, Pennsylvania, in 1980: he described her as 'petite, pretty, with long, light-blond hair, and wearing a tube top and blue jeans'. The girl then disappeared, but she had strangely left her few possessions behind in the apartment. Pascoe pointed this out to Sharif, who:

> realised then that Pascoe had been in his place without him knowing. He flew into a rage. 'If you ever do that again . . .' Sharif screamed. 'Get out!' Pascoe wasn't about to argue, and hurried for the door. It was on his way out that he saw a new shovel, caked with fresh mud, standing against a wall on Sharif's front porch. ('MONSTER' BEATS THE SYSTEM, Tim Madigan, The *Seattle Times*, 1999)

Sharif's rage is easily explicable, whether or not he had actually murdered and buried the girl, for the privacy of his home had been intruded upon without his permission or knowledge. There was a clear stimulus and it evoked a clear, comprehensible response.

Examine now another example of Sharif's behaviour, when he was living in Midland, Texas, and, on 31 October — Hallowe'en night — 1993, invited a woman called 'Ann' back to his house:

> It was a large, beautiful place in a new neighbourhood on the edge of town. They entered through the garage, and when Ann asked to use the bathroom, Sharif pointed the way. He was waiting outside when she came out, and punched her when she refused his advances. He called her a whore and bitch, and raped her.
>
> Then he poured her a glass of orange juice, chatting amiably, until his rage swelled back up. She said he raped her again and again until the sun came up, each attack interspersed with kindnesses, causing Ann to arrive at the same metaphor used a month earlier by Judge Nail [in the deportation hearing]. Sharif was first Dr Jekyll then Mr Hyde, a monster not content to attack

her body. Sharif seemed to need to mess with her head, too. ('MONSTER' BEATS THE SYSTEM, Tim Madigan, The *Seattle Times*, 1999)

Set this alongside the description, from the same source, of his behaviour during the multiple rapes he committed on a woman called 'Lisa' in Gainesville, Florida:

Several times during her ordeal, she wished Sharif would go ahead and kill her, too, would get it over with. But then, after hours when his rage rose and fell like some evil tide, he stopped. It was as if someone had finally found the handle to shut off a faucet of venom. 'Oh, I've hurt you,' he said. 'Do you think you need to go to the hospital?'

Sharif's volcanic rage and the sexual violence accompanying it are not easily explicable: what is repeatedly inflaming them and then quenching them? Why are they interspersed with 'kindnesses'? Why does the series of violent sexual and physical attacks in Florida end with the utter incongruity of an offer to take the victim for medical attention? The victim called 'Ann' in Texas was puzzled by the same questions, and her memories of the culture she inhabited provided her with a metaphor to encapsulate this puzzlement and the questions evoking it: Sharif was a 'Jekyll and Hyde'. 'Jekyll and Hyde' is another fictional creation that is, like Dracula, more famous than its creator, for it forms a narrative eminently suitable for translation to an easily digestible couple of hours on the cinema or television screen. The force of the narrative of Jekyll and Hyde, like that of Dracula, is most powerfully conveyed through the medium of vision: to see the transformation on the screen is more affecting than to read of it:

Late one accursed night, I compounded the elements, watched them boil and smoke together in the glass, and when the ebullition had subsided, with a strong glow of courage, drank off the poison.

The most racking pangs succeeded: a grinding in the bones, deadly nausea, and a horror of the spirit that cannot be exceeded at the hour of birth or death. Then these agonies began swiftly to subside, and I came to myself as if out of a great sickness. There was something strange in my sensations, something indescribably new, and, from its very novelty, incredibly sweet. I felt younger, lighter, happier in body; within I was conscious of a heady recklessness, a current of disordered sensual images running like a mill race in my fancy, a solution of the bonds of obligation, and an unknown but not an innocent freedom of the soul. I knew myself, at the first breath of this new life, to be more wicked, tenfold more wicked, sold a slave to my original evil; and the thought, in that moment, braced and delighted me like wine. I stretched out my hands, exulting in the freshness of these sensations; and in the act I was suddenly aware that I had lost in stature. (*The Strange Case of Dr Jekyll and Mr Hyde*, Robert Louis Stevenson)

Robert Louis Stevenson (1850–94) is confronting questions about the mysterious mutability of human nature, and answers them in his book in a satisfying literary way. Dr Jekyll drinks a potion and is transformed into Mr Hyde. There is an external stimulus (albeit internally assimilated) and an externally visible response to it. Mr Hyde's moral nature, fed by the invisible springs of the soul or brain, is changed from that of Dr Jekyll, and this change is accompanied by a change in *physical* nature. Jekyll and Hyde are not truly one person, but two, as distinct in body and name as they are in character. We are satisfied by this resolution of the difficulty because it matches our expectations of human nature: that radical moral or behavioural changes in a single individual do not take place easily or quickly or without some clear reason.

The real-life narrative of Sharif does not answer the difficulty. The Sharif raping 'Ann' and the Sharif offering her a glass of orange juice are distinct only in moral and behavioural nature, not in name and body, and we can see no clear reason for the transition from one to the other, let alone for the way in which this takes place quickly and repeatedly over the period of a single night.

That may be, however, only because we are not observing the situation in sufficient detail. Unless we are medically trained our perceptions of other human beings tend to be only skin-deep. Literally skin-deep. A beautiful woman is called 'beautiful' because of the way our eyes receive and our brains analyse light-rays from the surface of her body. We forget that, in one Christian saint's anti-erotic phrase, she is also a 'sack of dung': there is a great deal of physiological activity going on beneath her skin that our eyes and brains do not perceive. But this is true not just of beautiful women, and it is true not just of activities related to 'dung'. Beautiful women, like all human beings, have brains, but under normal circumstances we observe what is going on in those brains only by indirect means: by changes that are, again, visible at the surface: in the skin and musculature of the face, for example.

But what if we observe under circumstances that are not normal? What if we could have observed Sharif's behaviour with 'Ann' not just with our unaided eyes and ears, but with scientific instruments too? Suppose that he had electrodes attached to his scalp as he underwent the transition from Sharif à la Jekyll to Sharif à la Hyde, and back again. We would then have seen, I suggest, the underlying neurological basis of his behaviour, and might even have been able to predict when the transition from one moral and behavioural state to another would take place *before* there was any visible sign of it at the surface of Sharif's body. And before Sharif himself was aware that the transition was about to take place.

But what is it that we would have seen under these special circumstances? Presumably, radical changes in the pattern or level of electrical and chemical activity in Sharif's brain: the neurological equivalent of a storm replacing the neurological equivalent of a calm summer's day, and *vice versa*. And yet would we not have merely replaced one mystery with another in making this more detailed observation? The question still remains: why would these changes have taken place? To answer that, we would, I suggest, have to undertake a more detailed examination still of Sharif's brain and its functioning. There are more sophisticated instruments now available than scalp-electrodes and the electroencephalogram, and they offer highly detailed, two-dimensional images of the living brain: X-ray CT, NMR, and PET scans for example (unpacked, these acronyms mean X-ray Computed Tomography, Nuclear Magnetic Resonance, and Positron Emission Tomography, respectively). With these newly developed techniques or others that will surely become available in the near future, the electrical and chemical activity of Sharif's brain could be examined in minute detail to reveal, I suggest, some organic dysfunction in his brain responsible for these transitions from Jekyll to Hyde, from Hyde to Jekyll. Perhaps the neurological systems that in a normal adult male channel sexual behaviour in socially acceptable ways are missing or weakened or damaged in some way in Sharif. Perhaps sexual stimuli are conveyed to and activate inappropriate regions of his brain, such as the centres responsible for anger and aggression.

The same proposed analysis applies to many more sex-criminals than Sharif. Remember Peter Sutcliffe and the female typist who was struck by 'his pleasantness, his politeness, and particularly by the fact that she never heard him swear, something of a record among lorry drivers'. Swear-words are a sign of anger or frustration, but Sutcliffe did not use them in everyday life. There was, in other words, something wrong with the systems within his brain controlling anger and aggression. We need not, however, take up the hydrological metaphor offered by Freudianism, and assume his anger was repressed until it became too powerful to control. Sutcliffe almost always released his anger and gave vent to his aggression under special circumstances, and there are very few records of his manifesting his underlying psychopathology in a setting other than that of a red-light district or a dimly lit city street after dark. Here is one of these rare records from Laurie Ashton, a friend from Sutcliffe's time as a grave-digger:

'I began to realise that Peter was staring straight ahead, totally motionless, like in a trance, for quite a few minutes; then suddenly he took hold of the handle of his glass, stuck it up in the air and crashed it down on the table. There was beer and bits of glass everywhere.' (*The*

*Yorkshire Ripper: an in-depth study of a mass killer and his methods*, Roger Cross, HarperCollins, 1993)

Yet even in this description there is no clear indication of what Sutcliffe truly was and was capable of, and I suggest that the Freudian analysis of his behaviour is wrong: there was no mysterious, mindless fluid collecting in the vesicles of his brain, rising in volume and pressure until it burst forth in a murderous geyser of blood-lust. He smashed a beer-glass in that public house, did not attack anyone, let alone a woman, and when he did attack women, it was only certain women under certain circumstances, and the attacks, however violent, followed a kind of grammar of psychopathology:

In a paroxysm of rage he stabbed her again and again, some 18 times, in her breasts and chest, her stomach and the area of her vagina – fierce slashing swipes, a terrible burst of rage which relented only when the vilified body was almost unrecognizable. (*Ibid.*, p. 95)

The wounds described here were *purposeful*, aimed at particular parts of the female body, directed by a brain efficiently absorbing and assimilating sense-data about the environment in which its owner's body found itself. Sutcliffe was not an obvious psychopath: few serial killers are. If they were, they would find it difficult to find victims and to avoid attention from the authorities once they had found them. This is not to say, however, that there is nothing objectively abnormal about serial killers such as Sutcliffe and Sharif. If, as well as the clean, regular-featured face with its neatly trimmed beard, Sutcliffe's prostitute-victims could have seen the functioning of their prospective client's brain, they might have recognised him for the psychopath he was, noting the quickening flicker of neuro-electrical and neuro-chemical rhythms that were prognostic of a red, oncoming rage. And some of Sutcliffe's victims, prostitutes and otherwise, almost certainly never even saw him, perhaps never even heard him, being attacked from behind in dim light or darkness with overwhelming force.

But even now there is no readily available means of clearly monitoring the neurological activity of those with whom one comes into casual contact. We rely, sometimes mistakenly, on the indirect evidence of facial expressions and the voice. As well, of course, as the eyes.

# 11. Eyes

*Ojo m. Órgano de la vista: tener algo ante los ojos. – El ojo humano consta de tres membranas: la esclerótica, que le protege y forma delante la córnea transparente; la coroides, que se prolonga y forma la iris, horadada por la pupila; la retina, sensible al excitante luminoso, unidada al encéfalo por el nervio óptico, y sobre la cual se dibujan las imágines.*

Eye. Organ of sight: 'to have something before one's eyes'. – The human eye consists of three membranes: the sclerotic, which protects the eye and forms the transparent cornea at the front; the choroid, which extends and forms the iris, pierced by the pupil; the retina, which is sensitive to light and attached to the encephalus by the optic nerve, and over which images are formed.

He arrived in the city at dusk. The coloured lights of the traffic signals seemed to be crystallising out of the thickening darkness, to left and right, everywhere. Like eyes, opening on his coming. (*The Eyes*, Jesús Ignacio Aldapuerta)

*Poner el lobo a guardar las ovejas.* Set a thief to catch a thief. To understand a psychopath, go to another psychopath. To understand the behaviour of the psychopathic chemist Abdul Latif Sharif Sharif or the psychopathic lorry-driver Peter Sutcliffe, go to the psychopathic writer Jesús Ignacio Aldapuerta, the *soi disant* 'Andalusian de Sade' whose most famous – or infamous – work is called simply *Los Ojos – The Eyes*.

There is an extremely ancient tradition in Mediterranean culture of what English most famously describes by the borrowed Italian term *malocchio*: the evil eye, or the eye that by its mere gaze can cast a spell of misfortune or disaster. Rumoured possession of the evil eye is sufficient to cause someone to be shunned or avoided, even when it is acknowledged that the individual in question is quite innocent of any conscious evil intent. The Italian *littérateur* Mario Praz (1896–1963), for example, the author of a definitive study of literary decadence called *The Romantic Agony* (1933), was a harmless scholar but was said to have acquired the evil eye by his close acquaintance with the œuvre of the nefarious Marquis de Sade (1740–1814) and his *confrères*.

Whether Praz ever included Aldapuerta in his minute and punctilious studies in literary decadence remains unrecorded, as does whether Aldapuerta himself was in possession of what the Spanish call the *mal de ojo*, 'the evil eye', but there is no doubt that Aldapuerta was conscious of the maleficent power of the gaze, whether literal:

I sat and gazed at her.
    She was, I would guess, about nine or ten years old, puppyfat-less with malnutrition and disease. I can't remember very much else about her, not even what her face looked like, only that her skin was very clean because of the post-choleric sweating. Perhaps I should remember more, because I stared at her a very long time, nearly an hour, but you must remember that I was thinking at the same time. [Jesús Ignacio Aldapuerta, 'Handful', p. 39 of the 1995 Critical Vision (Stockport, Cheshire) edition of *The Eyes*.]

Or metaphorico-allegorical:

It was two or three in the morning. He had felt the glass in front of his face grow cool, cooler, cold. The cars came less frequently, and sometimes the giant green cyclops eye of the traffic signal glowed on him for minutes at a time. (*Ibid.*, p. 9)

Or another way:

Cradling her in two hands, he walked over to the flak-hole in the fuselage wall. The moon rode beneath him, a negative pupil in a giant eye of water. He sat down on the edge of the hole, legs dangling over kilometres of emptiness, and waited, dandling the head in his lap like a child, for the impulse to come to push himself and her out and down to the black, unending sea. (*Ibid.*, pp. 24–5)

These describe, respectively, an obese paedophile gazing at the child-victim he is about to rape, strangle, and *eat* whole;

a crash-fetishist psychopath waiting for a twin-car collision that will deliver a severed female head to him for sexual play; and an experimental-rocket-aircraft-fetishist psychopath already in possession of a female head and about to commit suicide by leaping from an aircraft several thousand metres into the sea.

In the first passage, Aldapuerta, drawing doubtless on his own psychopathology, implicitly recognises the subconscious nature of the maleficent gaze: the paedophile cannot clearly remember what the girl looks like, for just as his mind has been overthrown and conquered by the will to ill, so his brain has been swamped by the rhythms of an impending surrender to violence and sexual perversion. The second extract from *The Eyes* is interesting for the additional reason that it is taken from a story that mentions goats.

Goats have long been associated with Satanism and the anti-Christian occult, and usual explanations of this association have concentrated on their feral nature and a possession of horns that links them ex- or implicitly with pagan deities like Pan – goat-horned, hoofed, and with shaggy-furred lower limbs – and Dionysus, lord of intoxicating ivy and vine. I suggest here, however, that an additional caprine characteristic has been overlooked: their possession of disturbing eyes. Goats, unlike any other common domestic herbivore, have slitted, vertical pupils in what are often unsettlingly golden or tawny eyes.

Their eyes are, in short, like those of cats, and we can easily see an association between the great cat *Panthera onca*, or the jaguar, and the crimes committed in Juárez. The gaze of a jaguar or other predatory animal is unsettling because it is scrutinising, probing, supplying information to a brain whose centres of instinctual aggression and attack are activated. Examine now ocular narratives from the lives of Sharif and Sutcliffe. First Sharif, and information from 'Lisa', a victim raped and assaulted by him in Gainesville, Florida, and John Pascoe, his acquaintance in New Hope, Pennsylvania. Tim Madigan again:

'It was there that Sharif threatened to kill her if she screamed. It was there that Sharif said he had done it before, and promised to kill again. Lisa had no doubt, then or later, that he spoke the literal truth. She saw the evil in his eyes. Was it Pascoe's imagination, or did Sharif become even more sinister as the months passed? There was the way he lovingly fingered his huge, red-handled hunting knife, the look of madness that sometimes came into his eyes.'

Now to Sutcliffe, and information from Gerry Douglas, a Glaswegian whose family Sutcliffe, before his arrest, had befriended using the false name of 'Peter Logan':

Gerry Douglas, young and unemployed, looking like a down-at-heel George Best with a wife and three children, was later to reveal an amazing incident involving Pete Logan. 'One night Pete was at my mammy's house,' Gerry remembers, 'and my brother William said to him, "Pete, you know your eyes look evil tonight. I don't know what it is." Pete just looked at him and said, "Well, I am the Yorkshire Ripper." We all had a laugh.' (*The Yorkshire Ripper: an in-depth study of a mass killer and his methods*, Roger Cross, HarperCollins, 1993)

What these observers of Sharif and Sutcliffe were seeing, I believe, was a gaze controlled and directed by a brain in attack-and-aggression mode – a brain operating at an instinctual, animal level yet still possessing human intelligence and insight. If one were to take a metaphor from metaphysics or religion, one might almost say that Sharif and Sutcliffe were *possessed* by the spirit of a predatory animal. This idea that men can be so possessed is found all around the globe and on every continent. In the Old World, for example, the most prominent predator was the wolf, and men behaving like Sharif or Sutcliffe have long been known as lycanthropes: wolf-men: werewolves. In Latin America, another predator is more prominent, and so anthropologists find the universal concept of the 'were-animal' taking a different but closely related form:

The natural jaguar is a predator whose appearance and behaviour, in the inventive hands of the shaman, is raw material for elaborating an infinitely malleable concept of man-animal and shaman-jaguar transformations. Differences in age, knowledge and predisposition mean that the jaguar concept may be interpreted differently by individuals and tribes ... The Desana Indians ... possess at least three different interpretations of jaguar symbolism: some say that the 'were-jaguar' is simply a human who has been snuffing [*Anadenathera peregrina*, the psychoactive plant known as] *viho*; others take the identification of the shaman with a jaguar at face value, by saying that a man merely puts on a jaguar skin; whilst others proffer the opinion that the 'jaguar' is neither a skin nor a real jaguar, but an 'essence' or 'state of mind', which enforces the individual to act like a jaguar. (*People of the Jaguar: The Living Spirit of Ancient America*, Nicholas J. Saunders, Souvenir Press, 1989)

Does this not cast light from a different angle on to the behaviour of Sharif and *Los Choferes*, allowing us to see fresh facets of their psychopathology? What they did was 'natural' in one sense, but wholly unnatural in another. It is natural for a predator like the jaguar to prey upon human beings, particularly for it to prey upon the weakest and most vulnerable of them. It is wholly unnatural for a *human being* to prey upon human beings like this, even more especially for a *male* human being to prey like this upon *female* human beings. It represents a warping, a crippling, a truncation of the neurological systems of intra-species sociability and compassion that seem to operate among all mammalian groups and that have reached their highest state of development among human beings.

And yet we arrived at this discussion of the interrelation of the animal and human behaviour by taking a false step, when we moved from the slitted, vertical pupils of the goat to the slitted, vertical pupils of cats. For the jaguar, like other great cats, has *round* pupils rather than slitted, vertical ones, which are characteristic of the smaller species of the family *Felidae*.

What the eyes of great cats like the jaguar have in common
with those of their smaller cousins is this:

> Jaguars, like all cats, possess a dense layer of
> light-gathering cells at the back of the eye called the
> *tapetum lucidum* [literally, the 'shining carpet']. Whilst
> this enables them to see better in the dark and be more
> efficient predators, it also means that their eyes appear to
> glow in the dark when a light is placed in front of them.
> (*Ibid.*, p. 161)

The eyes of jaguars are, in other words, like *mirrors*:

> Eyes are full of metaphorical significance for native
> Amerindians: they enable shamans to perceive the
> otherwise invisible spirits, they are linked closely to
> mirrors and ideas of reflection and they emit tears, which
> are often seen as analogous to rain and so linked to the
> concept of fertility. (*Ibid.*, p. 95)

Mirrors were an integral part of pre-Hispanic culture in
Central and South America – remember the god Tezcatlipoca,
the 'Smoking Mirror' – and have exercised a powerful
influence on Latin American art and culture to the present
day. Mirrors reflect and distort, fooling the eye into believing
that right is left, left is right, here is there, there is here. These
concepts allow us to add another allegory to the collection we
will gather in the course of this book. The crimes in Juárez, I
suggest elsewhere, could be described as a *Comedia de
Terrores* – a Comedy of Terrors. They could also be described
as a *Laberinto de Espejos* – a Labyrinth of Mirrors.

Who is innocent? Who is guilty? Who knows whom, who
paid what to whom, who took orders from whom? There
seems certainty only at the centre of the labyrinth, where
Sharif waits like the Minotaur, bellowing his defiance and rage
down the twisting, mirror-lined corridors that snake back and
forth but lead always in his direction. And yet even Sharif
shares, in a small way, in the shifting, shimmering uncertain-
ties of the case, like a face thrown back from the curved

surface of a sideshow mirror or a *mesa* seen far off through distorting kilometres of sun-scalded desert air. What is Sharif's full name? One can find several versions in the American and Mexican media: Sharif Abdul Latif Sharif; Sharif Abdel Latif Sharif; Abdel Latif Sharif Sharif; Abdel Latif Sharif; even – probably a 'Freudian' slip – Omar Latif Sharif and – surely a typographical error – Abdel Latif Sahif Sharif. And yet the meaning of the one element that remains constant – Sharif – throws us back into the allegory of the *Comedia de Terrores*, the Comedy of Terrors. Sharif is a serial rapist and killer, and yet in his mother tongue, Arabic, his name means 'noble', *šariif*, from a verb meaning 'to be exalted', *šarafa*.

# 12. Drugs

*Droga f. Cualquier sustancia medicamentosa natural o sintética de efecto estimulante, deprimente o narcótico.*

Drug. A natural or synthetic medical substance with a stimulating, depressive, or narcotic effect.

All languages seem to have a tendency to shorten long words in common use. In English, omnibus – a Latin word meaning 'for everyone' – became bus. In Latin American Spanish, *narcotraficante* – drug-trafficker – became *narco*. Druggie. But there is an irony in the word, for *narco* literally means 'numb', and Latin American *narcos* typically prefer stimulating cocaine to numbing heroin.

But, they might ask, why should it be otherwise? For cocaine is a Latin American drug, produced from a Latin American plant with a Latin American name: *coca*, or *kuka* in the Amerindian Quecha language of Peru. Cocaine comes from what in the classificatory language of international science is called *Erythroxylon coca*, meaning 'red-wood coca'. The Greek prefix *erythro-* turns up again in another scientific term: erythrocyte, meaning 'red blood cell'. Here nomenclature echoes reality, for a great many red blood cells have been spilt over red-wood coca. There are huge sums of money to be made from its cultivation, harvesting, and conversion into snow-white cocaine. And of course, as the Bible puts it, the love of money is the root of all evil. In the case of cocaine this root puts forth an evil of tropical luxuriance, heraldically profuse, poisonously green, thornily glittering.

Take, for example, the 'War on Drugs' waged by the government of the United States for so many years. This has been, literally, a killing joke. Leslie Cockburn's *Out of Control: The Story of the Reagan's Administration's Secret War in Nicaragua, the Illegal Arms Pipeline, and the Contra Drug Connection* describes how, to finance the freedom-fighters of the Contra-Sandanista resistance in Nicaragua, weapons and cash were flown to Central America from US Air Force bases on American soil. The book then goes on to describe how drugs were flown back from Central America to Air Force Bases on American soil. And should the hypocritical stench of that particular phase of the 'War' ever begin to fade, point your nostrils – cautiously – towards another. An ongoing one. The complicity of the American chemicals industry in the drugs trade:

> Heroin is impossible to control by indirect means. . . .
> Cocaine is a different matter, and it should be possible to
> stop its production because it requires a few essential
> chemicals to extract it from coca leaves and refine it.
> Cocaine production in Columbia is probably in excess of
> 1,000 tons a year, and this requires the importation of
> 20,000 tons of organic solvents, which is 15,000 tons
> more than legitimately required by industry. Along the
> way to the final snowy white powder, the process
> requires the solvent methyl ethyl ketone, and the
> oxidizing agent potassium permanganate. Columbia
> imports over a third of all the methyl ethyl ketone
> shipped from the USA to South America. Clearly much of
> this is destined for the cocaine laboratories. The
> Colombian authorities are also trying to control diethyl
> ether, which can be used in place of methyl ethyl ketone,
> and have not issued an import licence for this solvent
> since 1987. However, the police seize almost 1,250,000
> litres (250,000 gallons) of it a year when they raid cocaine
> labs, and estimate that each year ten times this amount is
> imported into the country illegally. (*Molecules at an
> Exhibition: Portraits of intriguing materials in everyday life*,
> John Emsley, Oxford University Press, 1998, Gallery 3A)

Nature abhors a vacuum, and the vacuum created by American consumption of cocaine sucks the drug north, some of it by air and sea, but, particularly since an American 'crackdown' on direct exports, most of it overland, through Panama, Costa Rica, Nicaragua, Honduras, Guatemala, and El Salvador, until it reaches México, the final reservoir in which

83

it will be stored before it is released on to the market of the United States. Some shipments of cocaine take to the sea at this point, carried off the Yucatán Peninsula across the Gulf of México and the Caribbean to Florida and Louisiana, Miami and New Orleans. Many other shipments, however, continue overland to the border and cities like Juárez. Juárez is the drugs capital of north-central México, the power-base of a giant cartel once run by a druglord called Amado Carillo Fuentes, who was described by one DEA report as being:

> extremely well connected within the MFJP. Reporting in March 1993 indicates that Amado Carillo Fuentes possesses MFJP Jefe de Grupo credentials for the special investigations section and has a gold colored MFJP badge. (From a 'Secret DEA summary of the cartels and their link to Gonzales (sic) Calderoni', PBS Online)

The DEA, many readers will already know, is the American Drug Enforcement Administration; the MFJP, somewhat fewer readers will already know, is the Mexican Federal Judicial Police. The drug-dealer Fuentes, incredible as it may seem, had official accreditation as a drug-policeman. But he could hardly have been described as a *lobo con piel de oveja* – a wolf in sheep's clothing – because wolves and sheep are hard to distinguish in the world of Mexican drug-trafficking. Just as they are hard to distinguish in the world of Mexican politics: the Mexican president Carlos Salinas fled the country in 1995 just ahead of charges for corruption and complicity with the drugs cartels. The tougher regime that followed supposedly led to the demise of Carlos Fuentes, who is said to have 'died while undergoing surgery to conceal his physical identity' (*Northern Mexico Handbook*, Joe Cummings), although he was already famous for his lack of a physical identity: 'No one knows what he really looks like'. (WHILE YOU WERE SLEEPING, Charles Bowden.)

By then, however, he was long established as a popular hero, one of the underworld figures known, in seemingly conscious imitation of the Mafia term *capo*, as *jefes*, 'bosses'. And just as there is a Mafia *capo di cappi*, a capo of capos, so there is a narco *jefe de jefes*, a boss of bosses. The title was borrowed for the name of an album by the northern Mexican band *Los Tigres del Norte*, whose name literally means 'The Tigers of the North', though *tigres* means 'jaguars' in Latin America. The album recorded by these 'Jaguars of the North' consisted of nineteen *corridos* – ballads – but of a particular kind: *narco-corridos*. Though the genre and musical idiom are entirely different, the inspiration is the same as it is in gangsta-rap: the lives of *narcotraficantes y pandilleros*, drug-dealers and gangsters. Lives that are often nasty, brutish, and short, but that are idealised by many of the youths of cities like Juárez, who are further encouraged by official disapproval of *narco-corridos* to see men like Carlos Fuentes as avatars of past Mexican rebels: rising from the people to inhabit a phantasmogoric world of extreme glamour, extreme wealth, and extreme violence.

There are huge profits to be made from any illegal drug – Fuentes was said to be earning two hundred million dollars a week at the height of his power and criminals will fight viciously for their share of the market. However, trafficking in cocaine is much likelier to involve violence than any other drug. Many traffickers are also users, and users of cocaine experience a deadly mix of emotions:

> Taking cocaine produces a brief and immediate period of intense well-being, exhilaration and euphoria. This can be followed by feelings of agitation, anxiety or fear, and even hallucinations when the user feels threatened.
> Large doses cause sleeplessness, hallucinations, tremors and convulsions. Paranoid delusions can lead to violent behaviour. Respiratory troubles, digestive disorders and sensations of insects crawling on or under the skin occur. The pupils become dilated, and heart rate and blood pressure increase. (*Drug Warning: an illustrated guide for parents and teachers*, David Stockley, Macdonald Optima, 1986)

Those initial feelings of euphoria and wellbeing unbalance the judgment and encourage the taking of risks, and the succeeding feelings of anxiety and paranoia encourage a swift resort to violence when those risks fail to come off. Combine this with the already violence-prone *machista* culture of México, and you have a recipe for spiralling murder rates: male on male, and male on female:

2 February [1999] Just days [after the death of another woman], a 17-year-old woman, eight months pregnant, was murdered, and her stabbed body was found on 9 February, partially buried in a patio under construction at her home in Cd. Juárez. It is believed that her boyfriend, also 17, murdered and buried her on 2 February before hanging himself the next day.

José Luis Durán Estrada, allegedly a drug addict, told his family before his suicide that his girlfriend, Paulina León, had left their home to visit her mother, however the family found that strange since she had not packed any of her clothes. Estrada's brothers found her buried body a week later, and the cause of death was reported as shock due to loss of blood.

14 February On Valentine's Day . . . Elsa América Arreguán, 22, mother of a six-month-old and a two-year-old, and five months pregnant, was shot to death at the door of her home in Cd. Juárez by two men who had asked for her husband, David Campa López. América was a victim of regular beatings by her husband, according to her mother. Campa is allegedly a drug addict. There are suspicions that the crime may be some type of drug trafficking revenge or that the bullets were intended for Campa. Two suspects remain in custody. (Ann Marie Mackler, editor, *Frontera NorteSur*, March 1999)

These are examples of the female deaths that have continued since the arrest of *Los Choferes*: violent, bloody, but not accompanied by rape or sexual mutilation. They are isolated, fragmented evidence more of a society's psychopathology than of an individual's.

But recall part of the confession of one of *Los Rebeldes*:

'On the drive there all the guys were sniffing cocaine and after about an hour and twenty minutes' driving "Charly" tried to make her take some, like with his forefinger and thumb he wanted to put the stuff up her nose, but the girl would not let him, so the guys were hitting her.' (*El Diario de Juárez*)

Here cocaine is working as part of Mexican gang culture: *macho*, violent, self-gratificatory. Even if this particular incident in this particular confession is, as I have already suggested, a fabricated one, it must be based on experience, must have rung true with the gang member or police officers who fabricated it. Coke and violence. Coke and murder. Coke and rape. They go together like Jesus and Mary. For if drugs can warp the mind, so can culture. Particularly that aspect of culture known as religion.

# 13. The Egyptian

The cultures of Ancient Egypt and Ancient México, as has been pointed out by the Norwegian adventurer and historian Thor Heyerdahl in his travelog *The Ra Expeditions* (1967), show many strange and thought-provoking parallels: pyramids; worship of the sun, stars, and anthropomorphised animals; funerary mummification; hieroglyphs; papyrus boats. Modern Egypt and modern México show fewer parallels, but one very large one remains: desert. Egypt and México – particularly northern México – are places whose cultures have been shaped by heat, sand, and dust. In some ways, Abdul Latif Sharif Sharif must have felt he was coming home when he came to Juárez to take up well-paid work for Benchmark Technology and Research. He must have felt this because he is an Egyptian.

Today he is *the* Egyptian – *el egipcio*. He has earnt this status by becoming the chief suspect for the Juárez serial killings. For some, including his defence lawyer, this is evidence of Mexican xenophobia. Serial murder, the police have claimed, is not a Mexican crime: it is something foreigners do. Americans, or naturalised Americans, like Sharif, *el egipcio*. After all, America is a Protestant country, Egypt a Muslim one, and surely neither is anything like Catholic México.

Surely? Not so surely. Islam recognises Christianity as being, like itself, a Religion of the Book. Christianity's book is the Bible:

And He [Jesus] shall set the sheep on his right hand, but the goats on the left . . . Then shall he say unto them on the left hand, Depart from me, ye cursed, into everlasting fire, prepared for the devil and his angels. . . . And these shall go away into everlasting punishment. (Matthew xxv, 33–46)

Islam's book is the Qur'an:

What will be of the companions of the left hand? [They will be] in the midst of a fierce blast of fire and in boiling water . . . and in the shades of black smoke . . . [They] shall surely taste of the tree of Zaqqum . . : and drink boiling water on top of it: indeed, [they] shall drink like diseased camels raging with thirst! [*The Holy Qur'an,* Surah, LVI 41–55 trans. Abdullah Yusuf Ali (1946).

These cultural echoes are not coincidental, for Islam was built on a foundation of Christianity just as Christianity was built on a foundation of Judaism. A religion exists to perpetuate itself, and it makes no difference that it should do so at the expense of the psychological health of its adherents. Indeed, damaging the psychological health of its adherents is one of the most effective ways for a religion to increase its hold over them: it is the unbalanced who need priests (and *imams*), just as it is the sick who need doctors.

For surely the sadistic gloating seen in Christian and Muslim descriptions of the torments of Hell must have an unbalancing effect on those who are exposed to them, particularly in childhood. If God or Allah sees fit to apply His infinite wisdom to the task of devising ingenious ways of torturing guilty human beings through all eternity, can it be good for human beings to try their humble best to emulate Him?

The answer, for many Christians and Muslims, has been that it *is* good – so long as the cause is just and righteous, of course, and the tortured human beings guilty of the requisite crimes. Such as the crime of being female:

The government of Afghanistan is declaring war against women. The situation is so bad that an editor of *The Times* compares the treatment of women with the treatment of Jews under the Third Reich. Since the Taliban took power in 1996, women have had to wear a *burqua* (tunic) and have been beaten and stoned in public for not using the required clothing, even if it is just not using the mesh that covers the eyes. A woman was beaten to death by a group of fundamentalists when she accidentally did not cover her arms while driving. Another was stoned to death when trying to leave the country with a man who was not her relative. Since 1996, women [have not been] permitted to work or to appear in public unless they are accompanied by a male relative; women professionals such as teachers, translators, doctors, lawyers, artists and secretaries have been forced to leave their work and are confined to their houses. The resulting cases of depression are at an epidemic level. Women prefer to take their lives rather than live under such conditions. The houses where there are women have to have the windows painted so they can never be seen from outside. They have to use silent shoes so they can never be heard. Women fear for their lives if they commit the most minimal wrong. Because they are not able to work, those who do not have male relatives or spouses are dying of hunger or begging even though they have degrees . . . In one of the scarce hospitals for women, a reporter found immobile bodies, wrapped in their tunics, unable to talk, eat or to do anything other than to die slowly. Others have become crazy and are found rocking in a corner or crying, mainly out of fear. (Revolutionary Association of the Women of Afghanistan)

The Taliban referred to here are, of course, Muslim fundamentalists (although it should be noted that the concept of 'fundamentalism' cannot be applied to Muslims in the way that it can to Christians or Jews). Some Muslim apologists would defend the actions of the Taliban on the grounds that they are trying to restore the fundamental dignity of women in their proper, God-ordained sphere of the family and the home. The hollowness of this defence can be seen from a story that emerged from Afghanistan earlier, when the Taliban – as the freedom-fighting *Mujāhidīn* – were fighting for victory against a puppet government propped up by the atheistic Soviet Union. The story told of a:

> young woman living in the Shahrara district of Kabul in early 1994. Her husband had been killed in a bomb attack. She had three children of between two and nine years old. One day she leaves her children to go and find some food. Two Mujahideen armed guards arrest her in the street and take her to their base where 22 men rape her for three days. She is allowed to go. When she reaches her home she finds her three children have died of hypothermia. She has now lost her sanity.
>
> (AFGHANISTAN: THE WORLD'S DIRTY SECRET, *Amnesty Journal*, Jan/Feb 1996)

This is an example of what can happen when the sexual repression enforced by Islam on men is given opportunity for release. Other, less extreme examples can be found in the harassment faced by Western women in Muslim countries like Pakistan: the West is, in the perfervid imagination of the sex-starved Muslim male, a paradise of sexual delights, and Western women the concomitant ever-available *houris*.

Ever-available in every way. After all, Allah has ordained that, to her husband, a Muslim wife should be sheer tilth: 'Your wives are as a tilth to you; so approach your tilth when or how you will.' (Surah ii, 223.)

'Tilth' is 'that which is to be tilled', 'till' being a metaphor for the act of penetrative sex, and Fatima Mernissi's *Women and Islam: An Historical & Theological Enquiry* describes how this verse has been used to justify the sodomising of Muslim women by their husbands. There is, however, no little theological controversy about this verse, with some holding that it refers merely to variants on vaginal sex, and Mernissi's judgment is that the 'no-holes-barred' interpretation is a piece of self-serving Qur'anic exegesis by men and yet another example of the oppression and abuse of female minds and bodies that flourishes in male-dominated Islam.

But sodomy is a sexual practice that has flourished in Islamic countries not only against women. Islam has always restricted the access of the sexes to one another, and when the female sex is not available to the patriarch, the male sex will serve almost as well for this form of sex:

> Sharif would be his own star witness [during the hearing to deport him as an undesirable alien], insisting during emotional testimony that his mistakes were long behind him. Therapists were helping him work through the trauma of his Egyptian childhood, of being sodomised as a child by his father and other male relatives, Sharif said. ('MONSTER' BEATS THE SYSTEM, Tim Madigan, The *Seattle Times*, 1999)

Doubtless this is how sodomy has persisted in Islamic culture for millennia, as each generation's crop of male victims becomes sowers of the next generation's crop. For a male to be humiliated and psychologically and physically scarred by the act of anal rape by other males may, as we see elsewhere, be a potent ingredient in the creation of a male-on-female rapist. This certainly seems possible in the case of Sharif, for it could be argued that Egyptian sodomy was exported by one Muslim male for use against the Catholic women of México. And not only the fully grown women:

> The body of Irma Angélica Rosales Lozano, 13, was found in a vacant lot near the Luis Olague colonia on the southwest side of Cd. Juárez. She was raped vaginally and rectally, and suffocated with a plastic grocery bag. She had been released from work at Electrocomponentes de México, a nearby *maquila*, the same morning she was found dead. It is believed she had been dead for only a few hours when she was found which indicates that this crime happened in broad daylight. Semen was found in her body which has provided some leads in solving the

crime. (BORDER REACTS TO 184 MURDERED WOMEN, Anne Marie
Mackler, *Frontera NorteSur*, March 1999)

This particular murder took place after Sharif's arrest, but
anal rape is believed to have been a characteristic feature of
the sex-murders he is accused of and was, while still free,
capable of committing. This *modus operandi* would naturally,
if the police claims of an outside conspiracy are to be
believed, have been adopted by the proxies he appointed to
continue the murders in his name. These proxies would have
been Christians, but with attitudes towards women that had
been similarly warped by their religious upbringing. Examine,
for example, an interesting theory to emerge (albeit jocularly)
from the work of an American government commission on the
effects of pornography in the United States:

> [The campaign against pornography was more difficult]
> in Los Angeles, where the porn industry fought back
> through Beverly Hills lawyer John Weston, representing
> the Adult Film Association. Weston had done a little
> research of his own: why, he wanted to know, was the
> Commission worried about pornography when most
> serial killers in the United States actually come from
> rural, right-wing, fundamentalist protestant
> backgrounds, where their reading matter would have
> been mainly limited to the Bible in their early years?
> 'Would one literally extrapolate from that undeniable fact
> that the Bible or formal fundamentalist protestant
> theology inculcates within its adherents the desire or
> necessity of serial killing? I think not.' (*Soft Core: Moral
> Crusades against Pornography in Britain and America*, Bill
> Thompson)

But why not? Though it was invented jocularly, there seems
no reason for the theory not to be applied seriously. There
may well be a causal link between the reading of the Bible and
the sex-murder of women, for a constant theme of the Bible
is that of the sexually wanton woman who must be punished
for her misbehaviour:

Thus saith the Lord God: Because thy filthiness was
poured out, and thy nakedness discovered through thy
whoredoms with thy lovers . . . I will judge thee . . . And
I will give thee blood in fury and jealousy . . . [Thy
lovers] shall strip thee also of thy clothes . . . and leave
thee naked and bare . . . and they shall stone thee, and
thrust thee through with their swords . . . I will do these
things unto thee, because thou hast gone a whoring [sic]
after the heathen . . . Thou shalt be filled with
drunkenness and sorrow, with the cup of astonishment
and desolation . . . Thou shalt drink it and suck it out,
and thou shalt break the sherds thereof, and pluck off
thine own breasts: for I have spoken it, saith the Lord
God. (Ezekiel xvi, 36–40 & xxiii, 30–34)

In the Bible one can find a psychotic harping on the
promiscuity and lust of women, startlingly expressed in these
verses from Proverbs:

xxx, 15; The leech has two daughters, saying, 'Give!
Give!' Three things are insatiable, and a fourth that never
says, 'That is enough.' xxx, 16; Hell, and the mouth of
the womb, and the earth that is never filled with water,
and fire truly never says, 'That is enough.' (Translation of
the Catholic *Vulgate*, or Latin Bible)

The 'mouth of the womb', or *os vulvæ*, is, of course, the
vagina. These Biblical messages about female nature are found
in all modern versions of the Bible, but there are additional
messages in the Catholic Bible, which incorporates the Jewish
Apocrypha and includes another indirect but unmistakable
reference to the insatiable greed of the vagina:

A headstrong daughter must be held with a tight rein, or
she will find opportunity to bestow her favours . . . No
stake but she will make fast by it, no arrow comes amiss
to her archery. (Ecclesiastes, xxvi, 13 & 15)

This is the delicate mistranslation of the prudish Catholic
writer Mgr Ronald Knox (1888–1957), renowned for his

scholarship but unable, apparently, to recall here that the Graeco-Latin word *pharetra* should be translated not 'archery' but 'quiver'. When the word is translated correctly, it becomes obvious that Ecclesiastes is describing the woman's desire for her vagina to be penetrated by a penis – the 'stake' and the 'arrow'.

It is easy to imagine that such Biblical verses – the 'plucking off' of breasts, the 'tight rein' for would-be promiscuous young women – could become converted in the mind of a psychopath into divine commands for the mutilation and asphyxiation of female sinners:

Also, the left breast of at least one was mutilated, similar to some of the earlier cases . . . She was raped, vaginally and rectally, and suffocated with a plastic grocery bag.
[BORDER REACTS TO 184 MURDERED WOMEN, Anne Marie Mackler, *Frontera NorteSur*, March 1999.]

When Sharif emigrated to Juárez, he brought the psycho-pathology of one daughter of Judaism, Islam, into a region steeped in the psychopathology of another, Roman Ca-tholicism. The mix was potent, seething, corrosive, lethal, and destined to eat out permanent scars in the psychic landscape of northern México. Or so Sharif's arrest and conviction for the murders of young women would seem to force us to believe. This Egyptian immigrant Sharif, the police and media of Juárez proclaimed, was guilty of these horrifyingly brutal, radically un-Mexican sexual crimes.

And the belief in his guilt can only have been confirmed when it was discovered that Sharif had previous convictions for rape and sexual assault arising from his stay in the American states of Florida and Texas: in 1981 he was sentenced to forty-five days' imprisonment for 'assault and battery' in North Palm Beach, Gainesville, Florida, and in 1983 he was sentenced to twelve years' imprisonment for rape in Gainesville, also in Florida. After serving six years of this sentence, he was again released early, and was sent by the American company he worked for to supervise the setting up of a *maquiladora* in Juárez. In other words, he raped in the

*The probabilities of S.S's guilt.*

United States, was imprisoned, released, began to rape again in the United States, was imprisoned, released, and began to rape yet again, in México. But this time he also began to murder.

Or did he? For here we need to pause and examine a little-discussed and less-publicised point of statistical jurisprudence. Is the probability of Sharif's guilt strengthened by the discovery of his previous convictions for sexual violence and assault? At first glance the answer clearly seems to be yes. But is it? In fact, the answer is not so simple. One needs to distinguish between these two questions: Given that Sharif is the man responsible for the sex-murders in Juárez, how likely is it that he has a history of rape and sexual violence against women? And: Given that Sharif has a history of rape and sexual violence against women, how likely is it that he is the man responsible for the Juárez sex-murders?

Whatever the probability given for question one, the probability given for question two must be lower. To see why, examine these parallel questions: Given that someone is Mexican, how likely is it that he or she speaks Spanish? And: Given that someone speaks Spanish, how likely is it that he or she is Mexican?

In this recast form, the underlying propositions lose their initial obscuring emotiveness and become exercises in logic and mathematics. It is more likely that a Mexican speaks Spanish than it is that someone who speaks Spanish is a Mexican. Similarly, it is more likely for someone who is a sex-murderer to have convictions for rape than it is for someone who has convictions for rape to be a sex-murderer. The likelihood of Sharif's guilt is not greatly increased by the discovery that he has a history of rape and sexual violence against women. No one, for example, would regard a failure to discover such a history as greatly increasing the chances of his innocence, and Sharif's previous convictions remain circumstantial evidence of his present guilt, even in the face of claims made by a previous victim. An American victim:

Then, in March 1983, a 20-year-old college student answered Sharif's ad for a live-in housekeeper. Sharif

attacked the woman, Lisa, on her first night in his house
– punched, choked, kicked and raped her. And that
night, there was a particularly sinister element to his
behavior. To Lisa, he bragged of killing other women and
burying them; he threatened to kill her if she tried to
escape. ('MONSTER' BEATS THE SYSTEM, Tim Madigan, The
*Seattle Times*, 1999)

Such evidence must still be regarded as circumstantial, like
other facts about him, including, strangely, his intelligence
and, not so strangely, his taste for a combination of strong
drink and low company:

'I meet the wrong people when I'm drinking and I go to
the wrong places.' (SIX NEW SLAYINGS REVEAL THAT KILLER STILL
ON THE LOOSE, Mark Smith, The *Houston Chronicle*, 30
March 1996)

Sharif's own words. The pleasure and the sense of release
brought by alcohol depend on its effects on the brain. It
relaxes and dissolves inhibitions. It also, in Shakespeare's
words, 'provokes the desire', but 'takes away the performance'.
(Macbeth iii, 28.) The desire of what? As Shakespeare might
also have put it: the desire of venery. Venery is an interestingly
ambiguous word in this context, for it means both 'sexual
indulgence' and 'hunting'. Drinking heavily provokes a desire
for one kind of venery that, impossible to satisfy, may
transmute into the other. How many drunken men, frustrated
by their inability to achieve the gratification of sex with a
woman, have turned instead to the gratification of violence
against a woman? The erectile tissue of the penis is not under
conscious control: a man cannot bring about an erection by a
simple act of will. But by a simple act of will he can create a
fist, or pick up a bottle, use it to enact the second kind of
venery, and discover that he is then able to enact the first.

Was this Sharif's discovery? Alcohol has played a part in
rape and serial murder for as long as either has been
recognised, sometimes used to release the inhibitions of the
victimiser, sometimes used to enfeeble the victim:

And Lot went up out of Zoar . . . And he dwelt in a cave, he and his two daughters . . . And the firstborn said unto the younger, 'Our father is old, and *there* is not a man in the earth to come unto us after the manner of all the earth . . . Come, let us make our father drink wine, and we will lie with him, that we may preserve the seed of our father.' (Genesis xix, 30–32)

Lot broke the taboo on incest by being drunk, just as, as Brian Masters' *Killing for Company* describes, Dennis Nilsen broke the taboo on murder by being drunk. Drink seems very likely to have nurtured Sharif's psychopathology, perhaps even to have created it in the first place. Again we can see the lie in the claim that rape and murder can be pursued from a rational assessment of the pleasure to be gained from them. For rape and murder to take place there must be a psychopathic substrate, a temporary neurological imbalance brought about by a single bout of drinking, perhaps, or a permanent neurological imbalance brought about by the explosive physiological damage of a blow or fall, or the slow-burning chemical insult of prolonged drinking to excess.

It is the second, permanent kind of abnormality that underlies the behaviour of the serial killer, the criminal who rapes and murders not once but many times over an extended period. Sharif's brain was and is abnormal: I believe this to be objectively verifiable fact. And yet his brain is also a highly efficient one: Sharif, as we shall shortly see, has been described as a *mucho muy inteligente señor*: a very intelligent man.

But what of his intelligence? How is this evidence for his crimes? It is evidence for his crimes because above-average intelligence has been found to be a feature of a certain class of serial killer, perhaps best exemplified by Theodore 'Ted' Bundy (1946–89). Biologists have long observed that predators are more intelligent than their prey: cats are more intelligent than mice; wolves more intelligent than deer; predatory human beings more intelligent than the many, many species they prey upon – including the species to which they themselves belong, *Homo sapiens*?

Yes, it seems. Serial killers – those who make almost a profession of murder – have in some sense to be more intelligent than their victims. More cunning, certainly, but also, in the case of serial killers like Bundy and, perhaps, Sharif, more intelligent in the strict sense. Because they have to outwit not only their victims, but also the authorities, their employers, their families, their friends and acquaintances. Bundy was not a psychopathic drifter, but a psychopathic professional: he held down a good job while he raped and murdered. He could not allow his secret inner life to become suspected by those around him, or his secret inner life was over. (Perhaps, in the end, that was what he wanted: to carry out his final killing spree he is known to have deliberately moved from a state where murder did not carry the death penalty to one, Florida, where it did.)

And there are in fact some chilling parallels between Bundy and Sharif, almost as though the two were contemporaneous avatars of some misogynistic deity of blood and murder:

Bundy: Bundy scoured university campuses, student rooming houses and youth hostels searching for 'look-alike', attractive female victims. (*The Serial Killers*, Colin Wilson and Donald Seaman, p. 7, Virgin, 1990)

Sharif: The six most recent cases involve girls, ages fifteen to seventeen, who closely match the physical description of the nine earlier victims. All fifteen victims were in their teens or early twenties, slim and petite, almost always with long dark hair. (Mark Smith, The *Houston Chronicle*, 1996)

Bundy: His *modus operandi* was to use guile, plus his undoubted surface charm, to lure them to a waiting car. On 14 July 1974 he abducted two girls on the same day – Janice Ott and Denise Naslund – from Lake Squammish Park. Both were approached by a good-looking young man with his arm in a sling, who asked for help in lifting a boat on to the luggage rack of his car. (*The Serial Killers*, Colin Wilson and Donald Seaman, Virgin, 1990)

Sharif: In general, Sharif attacks women while on dates or approaches them, gives a fake name and states that his car is disabled. [Capt. Sadie] Darnell [of the Gainesville Police Department, Florida] wrote to [US Immigration Judge William] Nail on 6 November 1992. 'Once they are within his span of control, he physically attacks them, beating them severely, usually in the face, and rapes them. The [victims] were all verbally and physically abused. The detectives stated the victims were terrified, and said Sharif threatened to kill them.' ('MONSTER' BEATS THE SYSTEM, Tim Madigan, The *Seattle Times*, 1999)

Bundy: After his second escape from custody, Bundy deteriorated into a drunken, disorganised 'blitz' type of serial killer. (*The Serial Killers: a study in the psychology of violence*, Colin Wilson and Donald Seaman, Virgin Publishing, London, 1990)

Sharif: Not all of Sharif's colleagues, past or present, were so enamored [of him]. Tom Wilson had worked with the Egyptian chemist for three years in Florida, witnessing both Sharif's technical acumen and the spiral into drunkenness and violence that in 1984 led Sharif to be imprisoned for sexual battery . . . Twice in his first three years in Midland [Texas], Sharif was arrested on drunk-driving charges, but bosses chalked that up to difficulties adjusting from prison. Sharif insisted he had become sober after the last arrest in 1991, and was dutifully attending therapy and several meetings of Alcoholics Anonymous a week. ('MONSTER' BEATS THE SYSTEM, Tim Madigan, The *Seattle Times*, 1999)

Bundy: His background was far from normal. Theodore Robert Bundy was an illegitimate child, born in November 1946 to a respectable and religious young secretary, Louise Cowell, in a home for unmarried mothers in Philadelphia; his mother has always refused to disclose the father's identity. The child was left alone for several weeks before being taken into the home of his grandfather . . . When his mother decided to move to Tacoma (Washington), Ted was miserable at losing the only father he had ever known. (*The Serial Killers: a study in the psychology of violence*, Colin Wilson and Donald Seaman, Virgin Publishing, London, 1990)

Sharif: Sharif would be his own star witness [during the deportation hearing in El Paso], insisting during emotional testimony that his mistakes were long behind him. Therapists were helping him work through the trauma of his Egyptian childhood, of being sodomized as a child by his father and other male relatives, Sharif said. ('MONSTER' BEATS THE SYSTEM, Tim Madigan, The *Seattle Times*, 1999)

And it seems highly likely that many would-be serial killers are arrested and imprisoned before they can become 'serial', after one or two murders, being too clumsy to sustain a career that will lift their body-count of victims into double or even high single figures. Bundy and Sharif, then, embody a kind of psychopathic Darwinism, representing a survival not merely of the sickest but also of the brightest, the most able, of their monstrous kind. This perhaps has some relation to a strange phenomenon observed of murderers and serial killers after their arrest: that they receive fan-mail from many women, and even offers of marriage. The offers are sometimes accepted. On the same true-crime website on which one can find a self-claimed former fiancée of Sharif Sharif requesting up-do-date news of him, one can find the following message from the wife of a man born a stone's-throw from Juárez in El Paso, Texas:

This is Doreen Ramirez. After viewing several websites pertaining to my husband, Richard – including yours – I feel compelled to inform you that I am appalled to read the inaccuracies and, in some cases, outright lies, about my husband and myself. People who do not even know either of us are spewing outrageous opinions which they are passing off as facts, when it is patently clear they

know nearly nothing about Richard's case. I appeal to all intelligent persons not to believe everything which is being presented about Richard in the media. The facts of his case ultimately will confirm that Richard is a wrongly convicted man, and I believe fervently that his innocence will be proven to the world. Thank you.
(http://www.mayhem.net)

The phenomenon of women – even, as in this instance, intelligent and literate ones – being attracted to famous men is familiar with male sports stars and entertainers, and has been explained there in sociobiological terms by the evolution of a female instinct to mate more readily with 'successful' males.

Even when these successful males will not remain with the woman in question and allow her to use their success to protect her offspring. This may be because success is an indirect guarantee of genes for intelligence or dominance. The success of a serial killer seems likely to be an indirect guarantee of both: the intelligence to obtain victims and escape, at least for a time, the legal consequences, and the dominance to wish to murder in the first place. Distasteful as it may seem, serial killing can, like sport or popular music, be regarded as a career, a profession, in which there are famous successes and unknown failures.

This would explain well the interest Sharif has attracted from at least one female correspondent to the same Internet site just quoted from. Is the story she tells true, or a fantasy? Try and decide for yourself:

I found your site on the Internet while looking for information on the above subject which I know as Sharif Sharif. I was engaged to this man before he was sent out of the United States and got in trouble in México. I have had no contact with him for a very long time. When I knew him I had no idea he had ever been in prison anywhere. He suddenly broke off our engagement after a meeting he had in Houston, Texas, which I later found out had to do with his deportation and a law suit against

him and the company he worked for. I now know that he served 6 years in Gainesville, Florida, but was also convicted of a crime before that. I would like to know the whole story about him. What all he has done in the past, everything. I never suspected anything with him. He was always very good to me and my family. Since his arrest in México I have been finding out more and more things I didn't know. Can you give me more information on his crimes or tell me where I can get this type of information? I would really appreciate it.
(http://www.mayhem.net)

If the story is true, then perhaps she was attracted to Sharif because of another kind of success he displayed: he has been described as a 'brilliant chemist', with 'registered patents' for inventions made while he was working in the United States. The claim about his registered patents is certainly true:

United States Patent 5,565,513, 15 October 1996

Method and composition for delaying the cross-linking of water-soluble polymer solutions

Abstract

A stable, non-aqueous liquid suspension of delayed boron cross-linkers comprises an anhydrous boron compound or a sparingly soluble borate suspended in a mixture of mineral spirits (commonly termed as naphtha) and a resin. Anhydrous boron compounds suitable for suspension include, but are not limited to, anhydrous borax, anhydrous boric acid, or a mixture of both the anhydrous borax and anhydrous boric acid. Sparingly soluble borates suitable for suspension include, but are not limited to, alkaline earth metal borates, alkali metal borates, or a mixture thereof. The mixture between the mineral spirits and resin produces a mineral spirits–resin solution. Alternatively, the mineral spirits may be replaced with a suitable oil which forms an oil–resin solution when mixed with the resin. The oil–resin solution suspends the anhydrous boron compound or the sparingly soluble borate to produce a stable, non-aqueous liquid suspension of delayed boron cross-linkers.

Inventors: Kinsey, III; E. Wayne (Odessa, TX [Texas]); Sharif, Sharif (Midland, TX); Harry, David (Midland, TX)
Assignee: Benchmark Research & Technology, Inc.
Appl. No.: 495180
Filed: 27 June 1995

Sharif's name can be found on other patents registered at the United States Patents Office, and the income he is said to receive from them has been implicated in the charges of conspiracy brought against him after his arrest and conviction in Juárez. It has also been implicated in the *escandal de sus privilegios* – the scandal of his privileges:

Before this he [the procurator González Rascón] described a television programme that had been transmitted live the previous morning in the border region, during which he received a call directly from Abdel Latif Sharif Sharif that interrupted an interview he was holding with the special prosecutor Sully Ponce. (*El Diario de Juárez*)

It is possible that Sharif had been watching the programme on the colour television in his cell and, displeased by some point made during the interview, had rung Rascón on his mobile phone to protest. Possible, but unlikely: would Sharif have drawn attention to his possession of a personal phone in so glaring a fashion? No, more likely Sharif was unaware that the programme was underway (or was unaware that it was live), and simply availed himself of one of the many privileges he had while incarcerated in the *CeReSo* in Juárez: the ability to make unmonitored calls from his cell to the outside world.

When this came to the attention of the media and outside authorities, an investigation was undertaken and revealed the following list of items in Sharif's cell:

Photograph albums, newspaper and official clippings about the murder of women in Ciudad Juárez ... Two beds, one of them a double bed, the other a single, as well as a microwave oven, air-conditioning, a heater, a clothes-locker and wardrobe ... 14 video-cassettes, a cupboard set into the wall, a colour television, a video-recorder, a table, chairs, a tape-recorder, a bath with shower, a washbasin, a lavatory, kitchen utensils, and a place to keep them.

The Egyptian had been using a mobile phone to communicate with the outside world, above all as means of communication to debate with the state authorities. (*El Diario de Juárez*)

The list seems to convert the tale of Juárez's serial killers into a *Comedia de Terrores* – a Comedy of Terrors. A black comedy of bloody terrors. Sharif, mass-rapist and mass-murderer, was living considerably better in prison than the girls and young women he had preyed upon outside:

I am standing by the Carranza sisters' cardboard shack in a part of Juárez called Anapra. They moved to the shanty town about ten months ago, when three years of drought ended their lives in a village in Durango [in central northern México]. A half-dozen murdered, mutilated, and raped girls have been found about a hundred yards from their shack, and this frightens the teenage girls. Each morning they rise at 3:30 a.m., cook over bits of wood, and have some coffee. After a cold *tortilla*, they walk out into the darkness with their few possessions (a pan, a plate, knife, fork, spoon, and cooking oil) and bury them secretly in a hole; otherwise they will be stolen while they are gone ... The fifteen-year-old girl is a welder at 160 pesos a week (about $21.62 at current exchange rates). Bus fare consumes about half her salary. (*While You Were Sleeping*, Charles Bowden)

What was Sharif's income when he was free? What is it now? Another twisted laugh can be raised by another fragment of information about his life behind the bars of the Juárez *CeReSo*:

Fellow prisoners said they saw Sharif selling fruit juice and that he asked 1,500 pesos for orange-squeezing equipment. (*El Diario de Juárez*)

But this would have been small beer – small orange juice – beside what he may have been able to earn in other ways:

The general attorney's office of Chihuahua will send the Federal Bureau of Investigations (known by its initials in English as the FBI) and other investigatory authorities in the United States information about the correspondence conducted between, in Juárez, the convicted Egyptian Abdul Latif Sharif and, in the North-American state of Illinois, Newton Van [Drunen], who is serving a sentence for forging American currency. (*El Diario de Juárez*)

Another twisted laugh in the Comedy of Terrors is that the Chihuahuan authorities first had no idea that Sharif was keeping an archive of documents in his cell, and then had no idea of their contents, for they were written *en inglés y árabe* – in English and Arabic. Nonetheless, the female special prosecutor, Suly Ponce Prieto, was confident that nothing incriminating would be found amongst them:

'We are examining what the gentleman had, but he is no fool, on the contrary he has shown that he is an extremely intelligent man, so I do not believe that he might hold any evidence that could incriminate him.' (*El Diario de Juárez*)

But what of the things that seemed direct evidence of, at worst, Sharif's guilt or, at best, of his psychopathology: the photographs of women murdered in Juárez? They, at least, needed no translation, and seemed to indicate that Sharif had been gloating in his cell over the crimes – and perhaps more than gloating.

But this *mucho muy inteligente* man had an excellent excuse for owning the photographs:

> Sharif, however, said that he has become 'obsessed' with finding the serial killer himself. 'It has become a personal thing and I have studied everything I can about the murders while in jail,' he said. 'If the police and prosecutors would let me, I would like to help find the true killer.' (SIX NEW SLAYINGS REVEAL THAT KILLER IS STILL ON THE LOOSE, Mark Smith, *Houston Chronicle*, 1996)

In the same interview he suggested that the killer might be a police officer easily able to gain the confidence of young women, and that the renewed outbreak of murders might be because the killer was 'mad' that 'they have given me all the attention'.

And this was said, of course, *before* the arrest of *Los Rebeldes* and *Los Choferes*. Sharif seems to combine very dark sexual tastes with a very dark sense of humour. And with a criminal ingenuity that startled even the hardened investigators of the FBI, who announced that:

> 'The present case sets a precedent, because it is the only time on record that a sex-murderer has paid not one but two groups of people to commit sex-murders . . . A sex-murderer gets pleasure and realises his fantasies by committing crimes, so when Sharif paid for the murders of young women he realised his fantasies, as well as seeking to prove his non-existent innocence.' (*El Diario de Juárez*)

Another feature of the Mexican newspaper reports about Sharif is the continual stress laid on his *otherness*: he is referred to as *el egipcio*, the Egyptian, or as *el extranjero*, the foreigner. Perhaps the slowness with which the police and state authorities reacted to clear and mounting evidence that the crimes had not ended with his arrest is explained by the conviction that with a plainly guilty foreigner in custody, such un-Mexican crimes could *not* be continuing. Before Sharif's arrest, for example, explicit statements had been made to this end:

> One of those who offered his help during the investigation last fall – Rene González de la Vega, a criminologist with the México City Police Department – was quoted by some newspapers as saying serial killings are 'not a trait of the Mexican character'. (Mark Smith, *Houston Chronicle*)

While *El Diario de Juárez*, one of the main newspapers in Juárez, revealed that:

> That the murderer could not be Mexican was the initial hypothesis followed by the sub-procurator's office.

This belief seems to linger in media representations of those subsequently arrested: the name of Jesús Manuel Guardado Márquez is never introduced without his nickname 'El Tolteca', the Toltec, which is then the way he will be referred to in the rest of the article. The admixture of Amerindian blood in the Mexican population is reduced in the north, whose indigenous tribes have preserved a stricter sequestration than those of the south, and the sobriquet marks Márquez out as an outsider, a screen on to which the citizens of Chihuahua can project their particular form of a general Mexican racism.

*El Tolteca* remains irreducibly Mexican, however, but within even the culture of native Mexicans the name of the Toltecs has an exotic resonance, redolent of the commingled fumes of steam, smoke, and blood:

> It was not the Aztecs, however, who invented human sacrifice on the central plateau of the Mexican sierra. They partly inherited and partly assumed the mantle of a far more shadowy culture, known as the Toltecs ... Their principal city was Tula ... chiefly famous today for its reconstructed temple-pyramid of Quetzacóatl, the Plumed Serpent ... Gruesome indications of Toltec

rituals are to be found carved on a series of stone panels and free-standing stone sculptures . . . Marching across the upper and lower registers [of the pyramid] are a series of jaguars and pumas or coyotes. Alternating rows depicted crouching eagles tearing and eating the flesh of human hearts. It could be that these carnivorous creatures were fed human hearts after the victim's sacrifice, or they may be metaphorical representations of Toltec warrior castes dedicated to the jaguar or eagle. In other words, the Toltec warriors of the jaguar or eagle conquered and 'ate' their enemies, just as the real jaguar eats its prey. (*People of the Jaguar: The Living Spirit of Ancient America*, Nicholas J. Saunders, Souvenir Press, 1989)

And even if 'El Tolteca' did not have these associations clustered around his *apodo*, his nickname, and was pure, mainstream Mexican, the newspaper reports are always careful to stress his subordination to *el egipcio, el extranjero*, the Egyptian foreigner Sharif:

Sharif is identified as the mastermind of the seven murders and rapes of women committed by 'El Tolteca', 'El Narco', 'El Samber', 'El Kiani', and 'El Gaspy.' (*El Diario de Juárez*)

In Spanish, Sharif is the *autor intelectual*, literally the 'intellectual author', of crimes committed by 'El Tolteca' and the others as *autores materiales*, literally the 'material authors'. There is an ironic echo here of the Aristotelian theology of St Thomas Aquinas (1225–74), with its causes material, formal, efficient, and final. And yet no, there is more than that: the Mexican judicial system, like everything else in Mexican culture, is saturated with the influence of Roman Catholicism, and the most influential philosopher in Roman Catholicism is St Thomas Aquinas.

In either case, the irony arises from the fact that concepts from Catholicism are being applied to Sharif, for it is with Sharif that the indigenous racism of México commingles with a racism imported centuries before from Spain. Doubtless Mexican newspaper reports would be stressing the *extranjeria*, the foreignness, of Sharif if he were Colombian or Peruvian, but if he were Colombian or Peruvian, he would at least be Catholic. Sharif is not only *extranjero*, but also *extra ecclesiam*: not only foreign, but also heathen. Many place-names in México, as elsewhere, commemorate historical events, but some place-names in México commemorate more than Mexican history. Travel downstream from Juárez on the Río Bravo and you will sooner or later come to the state of Tamaulipas and a city called Matamoros. This literally means 'Kill-Moors', or 'Killer of Moors', a hero-name passed down from the Middle Ages and *la Reconquista*, or Reconquest, of Catholic Spain from *los moros*, the Moors, a generic term in Spanish for Muslims.

Like Juárez, Matamoros (and an identically named city in the state of Coahuila) is named for a rebel-hero, the priest Mariano Matamoros, who was born in 1770 and died of bullet wounds in 1814. Whether attached to a person or a place, however, the name retains its transparent anti-Muslim meaning in modern Spanish, commemorating the violent prejudices of a violent past. Sharif is a Moor, a Muslim, a heathen foreigner representative of the wholly other, not a *matamoros*, but *matador moro*: not a Moor-killer, but a Moorish killer.

This concept – *matador moro* – carries the resonance almost of a myth or fairy-tale, a bogey-figure with which women might threaten their misbehaving children, something catching and amplifying the folk-memories transmitted to the Mexican psyche in the Spanish language, where *hay moros en la costa* – 'there are Moors on the coast' – is still used as a phrase of warning or caution. And Sharif, an ageing chemist, embodies something of this resonance of myth or fairy-tale. He has been presented in the Mexican media as an ogre, a creature capable of casting a spell of fear merely by his presence, merely by a silent glance:

> I was told that on the Monday when they [the accused bus drivers] were in the cells, the gentleman [Sharif] took the trouble to pass behind them very suggestively. He

did not say anything to them but looked at them as if to say 'Here I am' . . . It was plain to anyone, but especially to them – and they showed every moment that they knew it – that if they talked and said what had happened, they knew that Sharif was going to end up killing them . . . Victor Moreno Rivera, 'El Narco', was the one who most showed his fear towards the Egyptian. (*El Diario de Juárez*)

But is this account, given by the special prosecutor Suly Ponce, to be trusted? It fits very neatly into the half-completed jigsaw she and the police are presenting to the public. For Rivera was, of course, the one whom Sharif first befriended on trips made by Rivera to the *CeReSo*, who was first offered money to kill four young women a month, who negotiated the figure down to two, who smuggled 'intimate garments' to Sharif as tokens of successful rape and murder, who knew *el egipcio* best and might be expected to react most strongly to the unspoken threats in this deadly criminal's foreign eyes.

But if men react to Sharif's presence with fear, women seem to have reacted in other ways. As pointed out before, Sharif, like many other serial killers, has a perverted aura of success and dominance that some women find very attractive. In fact, Sharif, even more than his lieutenant Jesús Marquéz, is reminiscent of another ageing, deadly foreigner: the Transylvanian Count Dracula, who similarly evoked fear in men and fascination in women:

Mina Harker's Journal, 22nd September

I was looking at a very beautiful girl, in a big cart-wheel hat, sitting in a victoria outside Guilano's, when I felt Jonathan clutch my arm so tight that he hurt me, and he said under his breath, 'My God!' . . . He was very pale, and his eyes seemed bulging out as, half in terror and half in amazement, he gazed at a tall, thin man, with a beaky nose and black moustache and pointed beard, who was also observing the pretty girl. He was looking at her so hard that he did not see either of us, and so I had a good view of him. His face was not a good face; it was hard, and cruel, and sensual, and his big white teeth, that looked all the whiter because his lips were so red, were pointed like an animal's. (Chapter XIII)

A tall man with a moustache who is able to cast a spell of menace by his mere presence:

Sharif bolted from his chair, towering over shorter guards who nervously reached for their guns. He was a large, menacing presence who filled the room, a man completely in control, against whom even the prison director seemed cowed . . .

'Man, you're pretty,' said Sharif, as he introduced himself to the girls. The tall, ruggedly built guy with short, dark hair and a mustache often followed up with an invitation. 'How about coming over to my place for a drink?' ('MONSTER' BEATS THE SYSTEM, Tim Madigan, The Seattle Times, 1999)

These are, respectively, a description of Sharif on trial for murder in Juárez and a description of him flirting with young American girls when he lived in New Hope, Pennsylvania. Examine further the startling facts uncovered by the inquiry into Sharif's relations with *Los Choferes*:

The director of the Centre for the Social Rehabilitation of Adults [or *CeReSo*] said that . . . the first person who had visited the foreigner in prison was a woman called Carolina who was signed in on the 15th of October, 1996 . . . The majority of those who come to the *CeReSo* to visit Latif Sharif are women and sign in as female friends of his. (*El Diario de Juárez*)

The Spanish is *se registran como sus amigas* – 'sign in as female friends of his': as female friends of a man imprisoned for the rape, torture, mutilation, and murder of an unknown number of other women. There is even a possibility that they came to prison to have sex with him: remember that among he items found in his cell during the investigation into his privileges were: 'Two beds, one of them a double bed, the other a single'.

The tale of Sharif's privileges seems to have become inflated as it travelled around the world, and one South African newspaper even reported that he: 'enjoyed extraordinary privileges in Ciudad Juárez's notorious *CeReSo* jail, including a fax machine, two cellphones and a water bed for conjugal visits' (The *Cape Times*, 17 May 1999.)

But the possibility that the women did indeed come to the prison to have sex with Sharif raises the further possibility that they were not *amigas*, but *putas*: not girlfriends, but whores. Sharif may have been hiring prostitutes to visit him in prison. After all, he had a mobile phone to make unsupervised calls on whoever he chose, and an income from, at the very least, the sale of orange juice and orange squeezers to fellow inmates. Another scene unfolds in the Comedy of Errors whose second act – setting: a prison; our Egyptian anti-hero is ushered into a cell – descends into farce as news of Sharif's extraordinary privileges fights for media attention with the news of his hired accomplices *Los Choferes*. When the prison authorities were grappling with the accusations levelled at them by journalists and reporters, one of the accusations they took special care to refute was that Sharif could ever have stored mementoes of the crimes in his cell after they had been smuggled to him by Victor Rivera Moreno. He could not have concealed intimate feminine garments in his cell because:

'We frequently make searches of the cells, and one of the things we watch out for most is that the prisoners do not have any female clothes, because they can disguise themselves as a woman and escape – it happened once – and definitely we have never found any,' the director of the *CeReSo* assured the media. (*El Diario de Juárez*)

But it would seem a very thorough female-impersonator who went to the trouble of acquiring female underwear before his escape bid. If he was suspected and searched for proof of femininity, the fact that he was wearing knickers and a brassière would surely be far less interesting to guards than what he was concealing beneath them. And dwell too on the picture painted by the director of the *CeReSo*: one of the guards regularly and minutely examining Sharif's cell, shifting microwaves, colour televisions, video-recorders, video cassettes, tape-recorders, and clothes lockers as they search for something suspicious, something out of place in the cell of a dangerous criminal in Juárez's notorious *CeReSo* prison.

# 14. Prison

*Cárcel f. Edificio donde están encerrados los presos. Fig. Lugar desagradable.*
Prison. Building where prisoners are held. *Figurative*: Unpleasant place.
'He did grind in the prison house.' (Judges, xvi, 27)

In Spanish, *preso* means 'prisoner'. *Presa* means 'prey'. It seems an appropriate parallel of sound and sense for life in a Mexican prison, for Mexican prisons have long been notorious even in the Spanish-speaking world for their brutality and harshness. Prisoners, *presos*, are prey, *presa*, of violence and disease, of malnutrition and corruption. And of sexual abuse:

> On the 14th of February, 1998, Juan Jorge Contreras Jurado, 'El Grande' ['The Big Guy'], a member of *Los Rebeldes*, led various other prisoners in a sexual assault on a nineteen-year-old internee who had just entered the prison to serve a sentence for rape.
>
> For this assault Judge María Catalina Ruíz Pacheco found 'El Grande' guilty of rape, along with the paedophile Javier Córdova Robles, Rubén Anaya Martínez, and Antonio Maldonado, for which they all received a six-year sentence.
>
> The victim said in his statement that 'El Grande' pestered him to have sexual relations with the internees in his cell, saying that 'all the prisoners go through the same thing'.
>
> Nevertheless, the youth would not give his consent to sexual relations, and he was therefore subjected to them by force.
>
> After the assault, the affected man decided to inform the prison authorities what had happened . . . Although the detainees denied the charge, the victim showed signs of sexual penetration according to the results of examinations given to him. (SENTENCE AGAINST 'EL GRANDE', *El Diario de Juárez*)

*Most rape victims => men =>
then these rape o*

'El Grande' undoubtedly spoke a great deal of truth when he told the nineteen-year-old that '*Todos los reos pasaban por lo mismo*' – 'All the prisoners go through the same thing'. Sexual assault must be a daily fact of life for many prisoners too weak to defend themselves against it. And that is true of prisons not just in México but throughout the world. In many countries, prisons are rape-factories, mass-producing male-on-male sexual assaults at every hour of the night and day on every day of the week. This fact, and the unimaginable mass of pain and indignity that can be inferred from it, had been mostly ignored – except as material for jokes – until it was realised that rape-factories can also be rapist-factories. The female response to rape is often internalised and directed against the self: depression and self-recrimination leading in some cases to anorexia and self-mutilation. The male response to rape is often externalised and directed against others: rage and a desire to take revenge. When those who raped him are beyond revenge, the raped male may redirect his anger against accessible targets, and seek to forget his own humiliation and degradation in the humiliation and degradation of others – others such as men weaker than himself inside prison and women outside it after his release:

> Blinded by their victim-centric view of women, the antipornography feminists overlooked the fact that most rape victims are men – and the fact that some substantial number of these male victims are likely in turn to attack women. According to conservative estimates, more than 290,000 men are sexually assaulted in jails and prisons every year [in the United States], while the Bureau of Justice Statistics estimates that 135,000 women are raped annually. Even if the latter figure is understated, as some critics charge, it is indisputable that there is an epidemic of male prison rape – an epidemic that preys not only on men behind bars, but also on women in the outside world. Consequently, according to Stephen Donaldson, president of Stop Prisoner Rape, 'the fight against rape in our communities is doomed to failure . . . as long as it ignores the network of training grounds for rapists: our

prisons, jails and reform schools.' (*Defending Pornography: Free Speech, Sex, and the Fight for Women's Rights*, Nadine Strossen, Abacus, 1996)

Such sexual abuse might seem to be among the many dangers faced by a sex-killer like Sharif, a middle-aged intellectual, when he was sent to prison in Juárez. In the hierarchy of prison-life, in México as elsewhere, the rapist-killers of women rank just above the rapist-killers of children. Both are at the very bottom of the hierarchy, recipients of all the violence and abuse the majority of prisoners above them in the hierarchy are able – or allowed – to mete out to them. Sharif could surely expect to be in constant danger of beatings, stabbings, slashings, scaldings, threats, contaminated food and water, and could surely expect to live against a psychic background, day in, day out, of the unrelenting hatred and contempt of his fellow inmates.

And yet Sharif, in another of the mysteries associated with his case, never seems to have been at risk from any of this. He seems to have moved freely inside the *CeReSo*, to the extent, as we have seen, of being able to sell orange juice to other prisoners. His height and physical presence undoubtedly helped him avoid some trouble, and the remainder may have been removed by his charisma. People had believed Sharif an innocent victim of injustice in the past, and may have done so again when he was imprisoned in Juárez.

Less physically imposing and less charismatic prisoners than Sharif, accused of the same, or much lesser, crimes would undoubtedly have suffered a great deal. But then conditions are bad for most prisoners in Mexican prisons, and what criminals find in prison when they are convicted are no isolated phenomena in the Mexican judicial system. Another of the twisted laughs to be raised by the Comedy of Terrors in Juárez can be found in the fact that the only one of the criminals to have made no complaint of police brutality and maltreatment is the protagonist himself: Abdul Latif Sharif Sharif, the author and inspirer of the crimes, and the man without whom they might never have taken place. Sharif's alleged minions, *Los Rebeldes* and *Los Choferes*, the men he is said to have hired and brought into the crimes, have all accused the authorities of torturing them into false confessions.

Each member of 'El Tolteca's' alleged accomplices among the *Los Choferes* was able to present his own story of torture and his own set of injuries to the Juárez media following his arrest:

### VICTOR MORENO RIVERA

He said that the police covered his head with cloths and after that poured water into his nostrils. 'With an electric riot-baton they shocked me in the private parts, they beat me, and kicked me all over my body,' he said. 'A man with light-coloured hair, he was the one who shouted at me to sign what he said to me . . . I felt afraid of dying.'

### JOSÉ GASPAR CEBALLOS CHAVEZ, 'EL GASPY'

Showing more than ten burns on his abdomen, severe bruises behind his left ear, and marks of blows all over his body, the twenty-five-year-old José Gaspar Ceballos, alias 'El Gaspy', said that he was illegally deprived of his liberty on Wednesday at 9:15 . . . 'First they kicked me in the genitals and beat me, then a police officer hit me with a torch in the head, here,' he said, pointing behind his left ear. The young man lifted his shirt and showed more than eleven (*sic*) burns on his abdomen that had been produced by electric discharges, he claimed.

### BERNARDO HERNANDO FERNÁNDEZ, 'EL SAMBER'

He displayed grazes on his right arm, as well as severe bruises on his abdomen and wounds inside his mouth . . . 'The police took me to the State Academy of Police and beat me. They put a plastic bag over my head and suffocated me, they also poured water into my nostrils so that I would confess to killing the women, and I did it when they beat me harder . . .'

### AUGUSTÍN TORIBIO CASTILLO, 'EL KIANI'

The last of the detained men showed a severe bruise on his stomach around his navel, as well as severe bruises on his shoulder and face . . . 'They took all of us to the [State] Academy [of Police] and we were put into separate cells with the police beating us . . . I denied everything they said I had done, but they were kicking me all over my body, and because they said they were going to "disappear" all of us, I signed what they said to me.' (*El Diario de Juárez*)

One might assume this physical evidence of maltreatment is good evidence of *Los Choferes'* claims that they are innocent men tortured into making false confessions. One would be naïve to do so. Like almost every other feature of the crimes, *Los Choferes'* injuries admit of multiple interpretations. Perhaps they are guilty men tortured into making true confessions. Perhaps they made confessions under some pressure, and were then handed over by the police to be worked over by fellow prisoners primed by news of what the men had been arrested for. Perhaps they even handed themselves over to fellow prisoners to be beaten up with the deliberate intention of making accusations of torture and brutality against the police. The idea has been circulating since, at the latest, the release of the film *Dirty Harry* (1971), in which the villain has himself beaten up to provide proof of an accusation of brutality against the eponymous policeman pursuing him.

And the idea – or an adaptation of it, at least – has been made reality in at least one prominent case of serial rape and murder:

The 'Railway Rapist' began to operate in 1982 . . . He threatened his victims with a knife, tied their hands, and raped them with a great deal of violence . . . In January 1986, the body of nineteen-year-old Alison Day was found in the River Lea . . . She had been raped and strangled . . . In April 1986, fifteen-year-old Maartje Tamboezer, daughter of a Dutch oil executive, was . . . also raped and strangled. Her attacker was evidently aware of the most recent advance in forensic detection, 'genetic fingerprinting', by which a suspect can be identified from the distinctive pattern in the DNA of his

body cells. The killer had stuffed a burning paper
handkerchief inside her vagina. (*The Serial Killers: a study
in the psychology of violence*, Colin Wilson and Donald
Seaman, p. 29, Virgin Publishing, London, 1990)

The man responsible was called John Duffy, and the
vulpine cunning shown by him here was evident again after
he came to the attention of the police and was interviewed by
them:

When the police tried to conduct a second interview,
Duffy was in hospital suffering from amnesia, claiming
he had been beaten up by a mugger. The hospital
authorities declined to allow him to be interviewed.
Since he was only one of two thousand suspects, the
police did not persist. (*Ibid.*, p. 30)

Later, however, he came to the top of this list of suspects,
and police investigations into his background revealed a
'fellow martial arts enthusiast' who:

admitted that Duffy had persuaded him to beat him up
so he could claim loss of memory . . . Five of [the
surviving] rape victims picked him out at an identity
parade, and string found in the home of his parents
proved to be identical with that which had been used to
tie Maartje Tamboezer's wrists. (*Ibid.*, p. 30)

This may have been the strategy adopted by *Los Choferes*,
and the possibility represents another bifurcation in the
*Laberinto de Espejos*, the Labyrinth of Mirrors, that the crimes
in Juárez seem to represent.

# 15. Desert

*Ruido m. Conjunto de sonidos inarticulados y confusos.*
Noise. Meaningless and confused sounds.

Tune a suitably old-fashioned radio to a spoken-word station.
Then, slowly, turn the dial until the voices disappear in static.
Then, very slowly, turn the dial back again. When do the
voices reappear? Is there a point at which they are there, and
yet not there? A point at which they flicker in and out of the
static like salmon fighting upstream in rapids, flashes of silver
in white foam, transient, meaningful patterns surrounded by
permanent, meaningless chaos?

I have just tried it with a suitably old-fashioned radio, and
there is such a point. A point of transition, on the cusp
between law and disorder, on the boundary between light and
dark, at the border between meaningfulness and noise. A
border reminiscent of another: that between México and
America. For the murders in Juárez are, it seems to me,
analogous to this experiment in mixing words and static.
Some of the murders are like static: random, unconnected
with each other, like separate grains of blond sand heaped by
the wind. Other murders are patterned: non-random, deliberate, connected to each other as part of a whole, like a
human bone lifted from that heap of blond sand. The sand
falls away in separate grains, and the bone is left in the hand,
white, whole, and meaningful.

The problem is, of course, to discern which murders are
grains of sand and which murders solid bone, which murders
the work of unrelated individuals and which murders the
work of a serial killer or the gang hired by him. Perhaps one
can apply again the concept of serial killing as career or
profession. Or, let us say, the concept of serial killing as *art*.
One can study the technique of a great artist and see
individuality, uniqueness, in the pattern of his brushstrokes,
in the deployment of his pigments, in the arrangement of his

figures, in the choice of his themes. In short, in his *modus operandi*: his method of working.

Like an artist, a serial killer uses his hands, and often instruments too, and he works on something analogous to a canvas or block of marble: the body of his victim. He often deploys fluids – blood, semen, spittle – or sculpts and rearranges his material with blows, cuts, scratches, bites. Or extend and modify this metaphor of art, and see the serial killing of Juárez as ballet: a dance of death enacted in the real time of real life, on a stage as wide as a city – because it is a city – and with a permanent curtain-fall for one of the partners in the *pas de deux*.

And see from this how, like an artist or dancer, a serial killer can so arrange the elements of his art as to achieve uniqueness and, in the ensanguinated terms by which some will willingly judge him, greatness. This has come to be recognised by the forensic psychologists, who have devised a system known as 'profiling' by which the evidence of behaviour in a crime is matched to personality and used to predict lifestyle or patterns of future behaviour that may allow the police to hunt down and arrest the perpetrator. This field was developed and has been brought to its highest pitch of perfection in the United States, where both resources and subjects for study are readily available. This American expertise in profiling was, belatedly, lent to the police and judicial authorities of Juárez:

> On March 8 [1999] three FBI agents are expected to arrive in Juárez to assist the local authorities in their investigation. The experts will be from the Behavioral Sciences Unit in Quantico, Virginia, and will hopefully be able to create a psychological profile for the serial killers and other criminals that may be involved. (BORDER REACTS TO 184 MURDERED WOMEN, Anne Marie Mackler, *Frontera NorteSur*, March 1999)

The FBI's offer of assistance was made before the arrest of *Los Choferes*, which came about by chance, not by psychological profiling. Perhaps this is because the murders in Juárez are, as yet, something unique in the annals of serial killings, though familiar in the field of art to which I have compared serial killing. Sharif, like da Vinci or Michelangelo or Raphael, founded a *school*. Even now some great paintings and drawings cannot be ascribed with certainty to an individual artist, but have to be labelled 'school of'. That famous 'human proportions' drawing co-opted for the British television series *World in Action* — the naked man standing legs and arms outstretched in a square and circle. Is it by da Vinci or a pupil of da Vinci? No one knows. Similarly, are some of the crimes in Juárez by Sharif or a pupil of Sharif? No one knows. And psychological profilers, working from the equivalent of half-a-dozen brushstrokes rather than a canvas-full, may never be able to differentiate such multiple-perpetrator murders overseen by a single psychopath.

Particularly when, as in Juárez, these half-a-dozen brushstrokes of which each serial crime is composed are overlaid and surrounded by the brushstrokes of incidental murders: pregnant women killed by their boyfriends; wives subjected to one drunken blow or kick too many; casual rapes turned into casual murders. There is a hiss of white noise through which a voice narrating a larger tale can barely be heard, a sentence scrawled in blood that is three-quarters-obliterated by a splattering of random gouts. Or a scattering of white bones in blond sand. When the stinks and colours of putrefaction have faded, the flesh melted away, and the wind heaped sand over the remains, it is sometimes very hard to find where a victim lies in the desert, and there is a great deal of desert around Ciudad Juárez. A very great deal indeed.

## Desert

*Desierto m. Lugar arenoso, árido y despoblado.*
Desert. Sandy, arid, and unpopulated place.

For he had commanded the unclean spirit to come out of the man. For oftentimes it had caught him: and he was kept bound with chains and in fetters; and he brake the bands, and was driven of the devil into the desert. (Luke, viii, 29) [I have followed the translation in the King James Bible, save for the rendering of *deserta* as 'desert'.]

National flags tell stories. The Mexican flag is a tricolour: three vertical stripes of green, white, and red. That tells a story of rebellion and revolution, for it was adopted in the struggle for independence in 1820 as a conscious echo of the *tricolore français*. But on the central white stripe of the *tricolor mexijana* there is a crest – a picture. The picture of an eagle. It is sitting on a cactus, biting at the neck of a snake that it clutches in its right claw.

The story here is harder to read, lying outside European culture and history in Aztec mythology. It is the story of the founding of México City, when wandering Aztecs were shown this tableau of animals and plant as sign of divine favour for the founding of a new city: an eagle, a snake, and a cactus. Two desert animals, and a desert plant. That the Aztecs chose them as symbols of their capital city, and the state of México as the crest of its national flag, tells us that desert casts a long, long shadow on Mexican history and the Mexican psyche.

Even so, México is not entirely a desert country: it has tropical and temperate rainforests too, in the south, and lakes and rivers in both the south and the north. In part, perhaps, the obsession with desert is a reflection of how others see México. And the most important 'other' is, of course, the United States: to Americans, México is a desert country because that is how it appears from their point of view – literally. Look south from the United States into México and you see desert, whether you stand in the extreme east, and Texas, or the extreme west, and California. The very names of these southern states – and nearly all their neighbours: Colorado, Nevada, New Mexico (Nuevo México), Arizona – are Mexican, for the United States grew at México's expense during the wars and border disputes of the nineteenth century. And these once-Mexican states are famous for their heat and their deserts, facts sometimes reflected in the names they were given in Spanish by their former owners: California was named the 'hot-furnace' for its climate, Colorado the 'Coloured State' for the vivid tinctures of its desert landscapes.

In part, then, México sees itself as others, including Americans, see it. And others see desert. But this might remain largely true even if the landscape along the border of the United States and México were lush green and humid, and Mexican deserts were further south. For there is something about desert that fascinates the eye and the mind. A vastness. A stillness. And an omnipresent whisper of death. A whisper that sometimes rises into a shriek. To look into a desert is to look into death. One's own death. Deserts are not places for human beings. That is why they are called deserts: they are deserted, *despoblado*, empty of people. They are too harsh, too fierce, for habitation, places to be hurried through or fought against from the foothold of a spring or well or river.

This is why they so fascinate the eye – or the lens. Films like *Romancing the Stone* (1984) or *Shark* (1968), the latter of which may have given birth to the first rumours of the 'snuff-movie' (publicity for the film included the probably apocryphal claim that a stunt-diver was killed by sharks during filming) were made in México but not set there, for cinematic representations of México, from the underground to the mainstream, are overwhelmingly of northern México and desert. There are Westerns like *The Magnificent Seven* (1960), for example, in which a 'Mexican village hires seven American gunmen for protection against bandits' (*Halliwell's Film Guide*). But perhaps the most famous films of this genre are in the short cycle that began three decades ago with *A Fistful of Dollars* (1964), continued with *For a Few Dollars More* (1965), and ended with *The Good, the Bad and the Ugly* (1966). The first is summarised in this way in *Halliwell's Film Guide*: 'An avenging stranger, violent and mysterious, cleans up a Mexican border town.'

The film created a sub-genre that would quickly coarsen into such titles as *A Town Called Bastard* (1971) (also known as *A Town Like Hell*), which is summarised like this in *Halliwell's Film Guide*:

Mexican revolutionaries massacre a priest and his congregation and take over the town. Ten years later a widow arrives seeking vengeance. Sadistic western with an opening massacre followed by twenty-two killings (count 'em).

The guide also notes that *A Town Called Bastard* and *A Fistful of Dollars* were, respectively, an all-British production and an international collaboration between Italy, Germany, and Spain. These films are México as seen by other nations, and other nations see México through American eyes, looking south to border towns set amid desert. Suitable places, and a suitable backdrop, for the enactment of the swift, bloody death by bullet or knife that symbolises the slower, dehydrating death always offered by a desert: death by thirst or sunstroke.

And here we find a further element of the macabre call of the desert. It will kill you but not destroy you, take your life but not always your flesh and very rarely your bones. The same deadly heat and sun may mummify you, sucking all the moisture from your body and leaving it unpalatable to the scavengers and bacteria that would swiftly dissolve and dismantle and scatter your remains in wetter, cooler climates. And even if your body is discovered in time by desert scavengers, they will strip your flesh but leave your bones to be bleached by the sun. The Mexican desert whispers death, and displays it, for white bones show up well against red sand.

As do black wings against blue sky. Death can be seen in the desert even when it is very, very far off. It can be seen in the sky, in a loose-edged wheel of descending vultures, hubbed on a tiny patch of death in the midst of desert *mesas* or canyons, *arroyos* or *playas*. All Spanish words, all taken into English from the Spanish of México. México is desert, and desert is México. Even to Mexicans. But Mexicans draw distinctions. There are deserts, and deserts. There is the desert of Sonora, and the desert of Chihuahua. And the desert of Chihuahua can kill not just with heat but also with cold:

Temperature ranges are extreme, varying from 40°C
(104°F) in midsummer to well below freezing in winter.
(*Northern Mexico Handbook*, Joe Cummings, p. 8, Moon
Publications, 1998)

Juárez is in the Chihuahuan desert. And however much its inhabitants try to shut out this fact, however widely the city spreads, encircling and shielding itself with shanty-town outriders in all directions, the desert's presence will remain inescapable. In Juárez the desert is never very far away as the crow flies. Or as the wind blows:

> I head downtown. A wind whips across Juárez. The city often sprawls under moving walls of dust since so little of it is paved. The whores are out, sixteen- and seventeen-year-olds. There is no way to tell if they are full-time prostitutes or factory workers making an extra buck. ('While You Were Sleeping', Charles Bowden)

In nineteenth-century London, fog cloaked the movements of the serial killer known as Jack the Ripper; in twentieth-century Juárez, dust has cloaked the movements of the serial killer Sharif Sharif and his hirelings. Even at a distance, the desert has provided cover for killers who will then dump their prey to its wide, gritty, dusty embrace. It is almost as if the desert has assisted in sacrifices to itself, swirling its substance over negotiations between prostitutes and kerb-crawlers, over cars driving off with prostitutes on board, masking struggles, confusing the direction of screams and cries for help, soaking up and covering splashes of blood by the roadside.

And later, when the bodies of murdered women have been dumped to the embrace of the desert, there is still work for it to do. For it and its master the sun:

> Jaime Bailleres has projected a beautiful black carved mask on the screen. The head is tilted and the face is smooth with craftsmanship. The hair is long and black. It takes a moment for me to get past this beauty and realise that the face is not a mask. She is a sixteen-year-old girl with a forgotten name . . . The girl's skin has blackened in the sun, and the face contracted as it mummified. She was kidnapped, raped, murdered . . . The lips of the girl pull back, revealing her clean, white teeth. Sound pours forth from her mouth. She is screaming and screaming and screaming. ('While You Were Sleeping', Charles Bowden)

The desert is waiting to do to all the inhabitants of Juárez what it did to this one young woman. If it can it will, in time, have all of them dead, desiccated, mummified, silently, deafeningly screaming to the blue ultimate iris of the sky and its glaring golden pupil: 'Juárez will run out of water completely in five years unless something is done.' ('While You Were Sleeping', Charles Bowden.)

And will something be done? Yes, perhaps. For the rich. Those who have. In the Mexican desert, those who have protect themselves very harshly against those who have not. Cactuses have water, for example, and protect themselves against those who do not have it with flesh-tearing thorns and spikes:

> The forbidding teddy-bear cactus (*Opuntia bigelovii*) has been described as being armed with 'ten million cambric needles, set on hundreds of loosely jointed spindles'. (*Wildlife of the Deserts*, Frederic H. Wagner, p. 165, Windward, Leicester)

The rich of Juárez have money, and protect themselves against those who do not have with the human equivalents of thorns and spikes:

> [A] paper [in Juárez] wanted a soft feature on the lives of the rich, so one Saturday a photographer and his editor strolled through an enclave of wealth looking for the right image. The photographer brought along his wife and two children. As a rabbit hopped across the lawn of a mansion, the camera came up. Suddenly two bodyguards appeared with AK-47s, and one said, 'Give me that fucking camera.' They forced the photographer face-down on the pavement with the automatic rifles at his head. Then, in front of his wife and children, they beat him about his head, ribs, and genitals. Police stood nearby and watched. ('While You Were Sleeping', Charles Bowden)

This savagery arises everywhere there is fierce competition for scarce resources, in nature or the human world. But in the desert there is savage competition *between* species; in Juárez there is savage competition *within* a species. Some citizens have more than others. Some few citizens have hugely, grossly more than many others. Juárez, like all of modern México, brings to mind in its income distribution one of the *teocallis*, the pyramids, of ancient México. But it is an inverted pyramid. A few, at the top, have a very great deal; very many, at the bottom, have almost nothing. Juárez is a desert of pain, where a very few have more water than they could drink in a lifetime, and very many have barely enough water to survive a day.

# ᵃ ᴾain

*Dolor m. Sufrimiento, padecimiento físico. Aflicción, pena.*
Pain. Physical suffering. Affliction, punishment.

'An hour of pain is as long as a day of pleasure.' [*Gnomologia*, Dr Thomas Fuller (1732)]

Have you ever lost a limb? Suffered third-degree burns? Gone a fortnight without food? A week without water? Caught smallpox, dysentery, or cholera?

Very probably your answer to each question will be a simple 'No'. The answers of your parents, and your grandparents, and your great-grandparents, would very probably be the same. The odd thing is that if you ever do have to experience one of these things, your body will know what to do. Only this is not so odd. Climb the tree of your direct ancestors and you will sooner or later find someone who did have to experience one of those things. And who survived and had children. Sooner or later you will find someone else who had to experience another of those things. And who survived and had children. And someone else who had to experience yet another of those things. And who survived and had children. And so on for each and every one of those things, many, many times over, stretching back beyond human beings into primitive hominids, primitive primates and insectivores, primitive mammals, and on, back into reptiles, fish, worms, unicellular organisms.

And that is why your body – and mine – knows what to do if it experiences life-threatening injury or deprivation or disease. Ancestors are, by definition, people who survived and had children. Their bodies knew what to do when the world attacked them. If their bodies had not known what to do, then they would have died and not had children. But they did not die and they did have children. And those children, and *their* children, and *their* children, already had, at birth, that implicit bodily wisdom bequeathed them by their parents, and *their* parents, and *their* parents.

As well as something perhaps even more important. For even someone whose body knows how to react to life-threatening injury and disease is better off avoiding them. Injury and disease are physiologically costly, and though they may not end life they may shorten it, and so lessen the number and quality of one's offspring. The safest thing is to avoid injury and disease, and the best way to avoid them is an ability to experience pain:

> People who are born without the ability to feel pain
> provide convincing testimony on the value of pain . . .
> Many of these people sustain extensive burns, bruises
> and lacerations during childhood, frequently bite deep
> into their tongue while chewing food, and learn only
> with difficulty to avoid inflicting severe wounds on
> themselves . . . [One] man walked on a leg with a
> cracked bone until it broke completely. Children who
> are congenitally insensitive to pain sometimes pull their
> own teeth out and have on occasion even pushed their
> eyeballs out of their sockets. (*The Puzzle of Pain*, Ronald
> Melzack, p. 15, Penguin, 1977)

Pain helps us to avoid injury by informing us when it is about to begin. It gives us time to react, sometimes *forces* us to react against our will, or before our will can come into play. Our bodies have been built by evolution to supply us, when the need arises, with inexhaustible supplies of pain in many, many different varieties and degrees.

And this is, in some ways, the most horrifying thing about being alive and conscious. Because if our bodies supply us with pain when the need arises, they also supply it when the need does not. When it serves no purpose. Pain is a blindfold gamble played by evolution with the lives of individual animals. Most of the time, the gamble pays off: pain helps an animal survive and breed. Some of the time, the gamble fails. A very young gazelle is caught by an inexperienced cheetah. It is doomed. Pain can no longer provide it with any possible benefit. The cheetah does not kill it cleanly, and begins chewing into its bowels before it is dead. Before it dies the gazelle's body supplies its consciousness with pain that is enormous and utterly useless.

And something similar may await the cheetah at the end of its life. It may have bred many times, been as successful as it could possibly be, but the taps of pain in its body will never be turned off. Finally too old and slow to respond to the spur of hunger pangs, it will nevertheless suffer them, and suffer what comes after them as it slowly starves to death. Examples can be multiplied from nature almost *ad infinitum*, certainly *ad nauseam*, and reach their zenith in the useless, unnecessary pain of the primates, whose evolution has refined the horror of pain in two ways, one of them previously unknown. Primates experience the most acute forms of psychological pain – fear, anxiety, depression – and were responsible for the invention of sadism: the taking of pleasure in the deliberate infliction of pain on other creatures.

Human beings have refined both aspects of this primate heritage even further. They have the ability both to experience and to inflict higher degrees of psychological and physical pain than any other animal in more ways than any other animal. In this, as in so many other things, we are, as yet, the *ne plus ultra*: the limit beyond which there lies nothing. But even among human beings, distinctions must be drawn. The ability to inflict and experience pain is not shared out equally amongst us. Some of us are men and some of us are women. Men are more eager to inflict pain for pleasure, and women more sensitive to its effects. The young gazelle with the inexperienced cheetah suffers greatly, but by accident; the young woman with the experienced sex-murderer suffers more, and by design. Those dozens of deaths by rape and torture in Juárez represent cases in which a gamble that has lasted for many millions of years has finally failed. A human body, exquisitely constructed to guard its own existence with pain, falls into the hands of another human being who derives pleasure from the infliction of pain. The victim's existence is effectively over. Pain can serve no further function, but the taps of pain are not turned off. The victim's suffering is enormous and utterly useless. *Lupus homo homini*. Man is a wolf to man. And even more of a wolf to woman.

Because the true sadist can have no better material for his sadism than the body and mind of a woman. Particularly a young woman. Even more particularly a slender young woman, with long hair:

The six most recent cases involve girls, ages 15 to 17, who closely match the physical description of the nine earlier victims. All 15 victims were in their teens or early 20s, slim and petite, almost always with long dark hair. (SIX NEW SLAYINGS REVEAL THAT KILLER IS STILL ON THE LOOSE, Mark Smith, *Houston Chronicle*, 1996)

But how do these characteristics – femaleness, youth, slenderness, long hair – contribute to a victim's suitability for the attentions of a sadist? Like this. The senses of women are, on average, sharper than those of men. Women can hear softer sounds, detect more fleeting flavours or odours, discriminate with eye or fingertip between more subtle colours or textures. If human senses are characterised as amplifiers, then male senses, by comparison with female, have the gain turned down: the output into the brain and consciousness is reduced from the input provided by the sense organs: eyes, ears, tongue, nose, skin.

This is likely to arise from the different roles assigned to the sexes by evolution: the care and rearing of children, for women, and competition and exploration, for men. And, like the almost universal human capacity to experience pain, it is written in spirals of DNA into our genes:

The twenty-third pair of chromosomes in females is XX, while in males it is XY. In the presence of the Y chromosome, cell division of the zygote is accelerated, and the medulla of the initially bipotential embryonic gonad differentiates during the seventh week into a testis. The secretion of androgenic hormones from the foetal testis organises both the development of the genitalia and of the brain according to the male pattern. Female differentiation always occurs in the absence of the male hormones. Circulation of androgens [male hormones] *in utero* [in the womb] is known to increase the amount of aggressive behaviour and gross physical activity in primates, and it is likely that these hormones predispose the human male to greater physical activity. (*The Oxford Companion to the Mind*, ed. Richard L. Gregory, Oxford University Press, 1987)

Greater physical activity increases the likelihood of injury, and so men are prepared in the womb to enter the world with coarsened senses, and sensibilities. They are less fearful of pain, more likely to risk it. And more *able*, with larger muscles attached to thicker bones, to inflict it.

These larger muscles on thicker bones account, in part, for the differing shapes and sizes of men and women, and the differing shapes and sizes of men and women, in turn, account, in part, for the differing sensitivity of men and women. Women not only present more sensitive bodies to the world but are also able to receive more stimulation from it. Imagine, for example, that human beings were shaped like cubes. A man might be a cube 2 m high, 2 m broad, 2 m deep. He would present twenty-four square metres of skin to the world for eight cubic metres of body. A woman might be a cube 1 m high, one metre broad, 1 m deep. She would present six square metres of skin to the world for one cubic metre of body. Her skin-to-body ratio is six-to-one; his three-to-one. Stimulation that saturates her consciousness merely dampens his; stimulation that submerges hers only soaks his.

But the use of large and small cubes to represent men and women falsifies reality: men and women are different shapes as well as sizes. The differing shapes increases the disparity in skin-to-body ratios. And a 'slender, petite' young woman has a skin-to-body ratio even higher than the female norm. As a woman she feels any stimulation more intensely, and pain is a form of stimulation. As a 'slender, petite' *young* woman, she feels pain most intensely of all.

But what is the significance of her youth? The significance is that her youth equips her to experience this most intensely felt pain for longer. Her body is stronger, more tightly knit, fuller of life and so slower to drain of it. Her 'long, dark hair' is an extra signal of this, for hair is one of the most powerful indicators of health and youth, or their absence. No matter what the currently fashionable hair-length for women, the women in pornographic magazines almost always have long hair. Its condition indicates their suitability for mating, and their suitability for mating is what places them in a pornographic magazine in the first place. Normal men are aroused by and attracted to healthy young women because healthy young women are likely to be more vigorous and pleasurable sexual partners who will bear and raise healthier children.

'El Tolteca' is reported to have explicitly stated Sharif's taste in victims as this was communicated in instructions to *Los Choferes*:

> 'We had to look for tasty little girls, with nice tits and asses . . . We looked for little girls, with properly developed bodies . . .' (*El Diario de Juárez*)

Healthy young women, by whom sadists like Sharif, in person or in proxy, are aroused and to whom they are attracted because healthy young women are likely to be more vigorous and pleasurable partners in pain. Though the partnership is not, of course, a reflexive one: XY is not to XX as XX is to XY. XY inflicts pain; XX receives it. It is not always thus in the world of heterosexual sadomasochism. There is a vast oversupply of men who want to be dominated by women: to be humiliated, tortured, made the vessel into which pain is poured rather than the vessel that pours it. To ensure the services of a dominatrix – a woman who will humiliate and torture them – many men have to pay. And many men have the ability to pay: it is a much-remarked paradox of sadomasochism that many rich, successful men, dominant and stereotypically masculine in their professional lives, wish to play the subordinate role in the bedroom. Or the dungeon.

The paradox may dissolve when we consider that it is also stereotypically masculine to seek out new sensations and risks. Subordination is a new sensation, and a risk, to a rich, successful man. Domination is a new sensation to poor, unsuccessful men. Perhaps this partly explains why serial killers – who dominate their victims to the point of death – are so often unsuccessful or unexceptional: drifters, road-sweepers, handymen, clerks. But we must remember that in some ways the greatest serial killers of all time have been politicians, with body counts not in the piddling tens and dozens, but the hundreds of thousands and millions. Their masculine hunger for new sensation is met not by difference but by increase. They have experienced the sensation of domination, and wish to experience the sensation of increased domination. Of domination in harsher, sterner ways, or in different arenas. From powers over life, they want to acquire powers over life and death.

This reasoning seems to apply both to men like Lavrenti Beria (1899–1953), the head of the Stalin's secret police and a monster in his political and his sexual life alike, and to men like Abdul Latif Sharif Sharif, a successful, dominant chemist and a successful, dominant sex-criminal. The two kinds of male sadist – the failure who seeks compensation for his failure, and the success who wants more 'success' – seem conjoined in Sharif's association with *Los Rebeldes* and *Los Choferes*. A rich man imprisoned for rape and murder pays poor men to rape and murder on his behalf. And the story of it reveals another strand of the way male and female characteristics have been woven together in the crimes.

Almost nothing is known of how Sharif captured and murdered his victims before dumping them in the desert. If the confessions of *Los Rebeldes*, and the testimony of 'Nancy', are to be trusted, Sharif's accomplices used cars and buses. The confessions of *Los Rebeldes* are full of street names, changes of direction, travel to and travel through and travel from. Journeys, in short. Something that bus drivers, by definition, make the most important part of their work. And men, on average, are better at making journeys than women: better at changes of direction, better at travel to and travel through and travel from:

Men and women use their brains differently, it appears. Women are not as good at spatial tasks, but they are better than men at dealing with complex verbal information. Psychological testing had indicated these differences, but now brain imaging has shown that they are caused by men and women using different areas of their brains when they carry out the same tests. (IT IS TRUE, WOMEN FIND MAPS A MAZE, Nigel Hawkes, *The Times*, 25th July 1999)

And so *Los Choferes*, The Bus Drivers, sorted into a driving job by their maleness, were brought into daily contact with *Las Victimas*, The Victims, sorted into factory jobs by their femaleness: their sharper eyes, more sensitive fingers, more subordinate response to authority and regimentation. Again the crimes seem like a work of dramatic art: a ballet or film in which roles were advertised and competed for, and central casting was evolutionary biology.

And yet a mystery remains at the heart of the crimes. The same mystery is found at the heart of all human existence and action, but crimes such as those of Juárez throw it into sharper, starker relief. Extremes demand and challenge explanations, and it is in the extremes of human behaviour that psychology and neurology are most strongly tested, and are in most urgent need of application. The mystery is this: what is the relationship between consciousness and action? Again and again in this chapter I have made an implicit assumption: that the contents of the mind drive behaviour. The pain of being raped and tortured makes a young woman scream, weep; the pleasure of raping and torturing makes a sex-criminal laugh, ejaculate. And the knowledge or the memory of this pain or pleasure makes it possible that others take action to avoid or re-enact it:

Before Sharif's arrest, many parents wouldn't let their children go out alone or after dark. Teenage girls cut their hair and dressed in baggy clothes to be less attractive to the mysterious killer. Juárez's busy nightclubs and restaurants reported a drop in business. (SIX NEW SLAYINGS REVEAL THAT KILLER IS STILL ON THE LOOSE, Mark Smith, *Houston Chronicle*, 1996)

The sex-criminals, on the other hand, seek out opportunities to snatch new victims, driven by the memory of the pleasure they experienced last time, or the desire to earn more money. In each case, we explain the actions by reference to the contents of the mind of the individual who undertakes the action. A teenaged girl is fearful of being a victim: she cuts her hair and wears baggy clothes. A bus driver wants another envelope of female flesh, another envelope of cash, and notes each potential new target getting on his bus, where she gets off. Question that teenaged girl or bus driver about *why* she or he does what she or he does, and the answer will be couched with reference to the contents of her or his mind: 'I did it out of fear, desire, greed'.

But in most contemporary philosophy and neuroscience, there seems no need to ascend to this level of meaning: the contents of the mind are effectively identical to the contents of the brain. Fear, desire, greed, and all the other elements of consciousness, depend on the arrangement of chemicals and electrical charges in the brain. Consciousness seems to float on the brain like steam on the surface of the boiling mudpools and fumaroles of New Zealand's Rotorua district or America's Yellowstone Park: it does not affect what goes on beneath it, and merely echoes changes in that from which it arises.

Why, then, does it exist? If the physical substrate of pain – its representation in brain-stuff – is sufficient, why is there any need for its psychological suprastrate: its representation in mind-stuff? Is the already certain horror of existence – that some pain is unnecessary – only a fragment of the truth? Is *all* pain unnecessary? Can consciousness be compared to a months-old European newspaper appearing at last in a decaying town in the remote Mexican *sierra*, reporting events that the reader can neither participate in nor influence?

Perhaps, perhaps not. But even if consciousness does influence brain-state in some as yet unimaginable way, its importance is already undermined by what has been learned by science about human behaviour. Some of those responsible for violent sex-crime have openly stated that they do such things for the sake of pleasure. The Hungarian train-wreck fetishist Sylvestre Matuschka, for example, is said to have announced, ten days after his arrest:

'I wrecked trains because I like to see people die. I like to hear them scream. I like to see them suffer.' (*The Sex Killers, Thirty fully documented cases of men and women whose aberrant sexuality drove them to kill*, Norman Lucas, p. 5, Virgin, 1998)

There is direct testimony that Guardado Márquez, 'El Tolteca', 'El Dracula', found a similar pleasure in the suffering of others, though at much closer quarters. After his arrest for the rape of Nancy, the Juárez media described how he seemed to drink in the fear of his underaged victim as eagerly as his Transylvanian nick-namesake drank blood. When he and Nancy were left alone on the bus she had boarded late at night to get home from her *maquiladora* job: ' "The Toltec" asked her, smiling, "Are you afraid?", to which she answered, "Yes, please take me home." '

Nancy then described her feelings as the bus droned on into the night, taking her further and further from home, further and further into the deserted outskirts of Juárez:

'I was very afraid during the whole journey, I did not do anything because I could not, my fear was stronger than I was,' she recalls. 'As soon as he had stopped the bus he threw himself at me and grabbed me by the throat very hard, saying at the same time that he was going to kill me, and smiling as he asked me again and again whether I was afraid.

'I do not remember anything more because I fainted,' she says with tears that testify to the brutality Jesús Manuel Guardado Márquez used against her. (*El Diario de Juárez*)

Here we find a perfect vignette of male pleasure in the heightened fear and suffering experienced by the female victim. The words of another young woman raped by 'El Tolteca' emphasise another dichotomy between the sexes. On average, women are more empathetic, better able to identify with the emotion and suffering of others. Once she saw him in prison, the young woman identified only as Susana said:

> 'I am afraid, but when I saw him I felt pity for him, though he does not deserve my pity. He did a lot of harm to Nancy and me, he killed many girls and he has to pay for what he did.' (*El Diario de Juárez*)

But in one way Susana could not identify with 'El Tolteca', because the feelings he had were alien to her. On average, women are slower to sexual arousal than men and are far less eager for as much sex with as many partners as possible. From Venus, Susana could not make out the depth of the canyons cut out by storms in the surface of Mars:

> 'Now, after seeing what he did to Nancy and me, I believe he did the same to other women. I do not understand why he did it. If he has a wife, why does he go searching for other women?' the victim asked. (*El Diario de Juárez*)

This average difference of sexual appetite between the sexes is a natural phenomenon, easily explained by the relative investment men and women have to place into what has historically been the consequence of sex: pregnancy and children. Over evolutionary time, female human beings have always risked more by having sex, and the brains and behaviour of women have been shaped accordingly. Men, on the other hand, can often lose nothing by sex but a few cubic centimetres of semen, and their brains and behaviour have been shaped accordingly. In general, women are discriminately sexual, men indiscriminately sexual, both adapted to seeking the best advantage of their genes.

But some would go further and claim that the vigour of the male pursuit of sex must, by the truly honest, be coupled with violence, and that it is only in this way that true pleasure can be found in sex. Remember the words used by Hungarian sex-criminal Sylvestre Matuschka to express the feelings of his psychopathic *confrères*: 'I wrecked trains because I like to see people die. I like to hear them scream. I like to see them suffer.' Some of the sex-criminals *manqués* who gloat over crimes such as those committed by Matuschka – or Sharif – would echo, and have echoed, such claims. Neither group is to be trusted:

> High P scorers seem pathologically drawn towards sexual behaviour which in the end does not satisfy them. They do not share the neurotic's guilt, and do not show any repression; nor do they show the neurotic's nervousness towards members of the opposite sex. Looking through the inventories of high P scorers, one almost feels that they are addicted to sex as if to a drug, and that this addiction and dependence creates more difficulties for them than it solves. (*Psychology is about People*, H.J. Eysenck, p. 90, Penguin, 1982)

'P' stands for 'Psychoticism', and men like Sharif and the members of *Los Rebeldes* and *Los Choferes* certainly seem to be psychotics whose sexual behaviour has created more problems for them than it has solved. What they or their *aficionados* might say about their motives is not to be trusted, for consciousness does not always tell the truth about the basis of one's actions:

> [A] subject is hypnotized and told that he will be awakened after ten minutes. He is further told that some time after this the hypnotist will blow his nose three times. Upon receipt of this signal, the subject will get up, go out into the hall, pick up the third umbrella from the left on the rack, go back into the room, and put up the umbrella there . . . When the experimenter blows his nose three times, the [hypnotized and awakened] subject becomes vaguely restless and uneasy; finally, he gets up, leaves the room, picks up the designated umbrella, brings it back to the room and puts it up. When questioned as to the reasons for his actions, he cannot, of course, give the true reason because he is unconscious of

it. Instead he will make up as good a reason as he can . . .
Many of these rationalizations are quite remarkable in
their ingenuity, and intelligent people in particular can
usually find a good reason for doing almost anything that
has been suggested to them under hypnosis. What is
more, they apparently believe their own rationalizations
implicitly. (*Sense and Nonsense in Psychology*, H.J.
Eysenck, p. 41–2, Pelican, 1978)

A rationalisation is an attempt to express the reason behind
– and the rationality of – one's actions. In fact, these may be,
as in the experiment just described, quite without reason from
the point of view of the individual. Not necessarily irrational,
but arational: not opposed to reason, but operating by laws
outside or beyond reason, unless they are taken in a wider
context. In a wider context of laws and police agencies,
sex-crime is not a rational way of seeking pleasure unless it
can be committed both without immediate risk and without
fear of later detection. An intelligent, successful man like
Sharif could have obtained legitimate, legal pleasures in
abundance during his stay in the United States, but ran the
risks of rape and violence against women instead. These risks
caught up with him, and he suffered the indignities and
privations of incarceration in the American prison system.
And perhaps, while he was incarcerated, he suffered rape and
violence against his own person. Now he is again incarcerated, and in a prison system even more notorious than that
of the United States. Was the pleasure he gained from his
crimes sufficient to compensate him for what he has lost?

And even if he replied that it was, and is neither
rationalising nor lying, try the thought-experiment of offering
him, or some other psychopath with his inclinations, the
opportunity to obtain, entirely without risk of possible
sanctions, more pleasure than he could conceivably obtain in
a lifetime – a hundred lifetimes – of unquantifiable sex-crime.
Try the thought experiment of offering him, or some other
psychopath with his inclinations, the opportunity of being
directly stimulated in the pleasure centre of the brain. This
would be pure, unadulterated pleasure. Any admixture of

sensation or thought could only dilute and weaken it. It would be available for as long as the stimulation were supplied, and would be available without risk and without physiological cost, for the famous stories about laboratory rats self-stimulating to the point of exhaustion or starvation are false: a self-stimulating rat will reorganise its life around self-stimulation, but not neglect food or grooming. But would Sharif, or a psychopath like him, accept this form of pleasure, given a choice between it and, say, a fresh opportunity to rape and murder a perfect victim?

Presumably no, he would not. He would understand the choice, but be unable to make it in the rational direction: that of direct brain-stimulation and greatly enhanced pleasure. Irrational, or arational, forces operating in his brain below the level of consciousness would impel him in the direction of indirect brain-stimulation through the sense-organs of the eyes and ears and genitals. For him this would mean greatly reduced pleasure. Pleasure that would be impure, tainted with sense-data and with what the American linguist Steven Pinker has called 'mentalese': the raw concept-stuff of pre- or sub-linguistic thought. (See Pinker's *The Language Instinct* for further discussion of this term.) The sadist is seeking power and domination, but these are concepts that are not in themselves pleasurable, merely tokens representing relation-ships between entities in the sadist's universe. To introduce them into the psycho-sexual discourse of rape and torture may enhance the initial pleasure, but will block its ultimate fulfilment, for it crowds the mind with information that might otherwise be devoted to the pure stuff of pleasure.

But the choice our hypothetical Sharif makes when pres-ented with a verbal explanation of its entailments might alter if he were allowed to *experience* direct brain-stimulation, and so was shown the incomparable pleasure it offered. Here he would, perhaps, realise the irrationality of his previous choice, for human beings are usually guided not by reason but by what they perceive through the sense organs. By what they hear and taste and smell and feel. And by what they see.

# 17. Light

*Luz f. Lo que ilumina los objetos y les hace visibles.*
Light. That which illuminates objects and makes them visible.

*Fiat lux*. Let there be light. (Genesis, i, 3)

It is a well-established rule that wherever visual technology goes, pornography is breathing hotly down its neck. This is as true today with the World Wide Web as it was back in 1839 when reliable photography was first developed. And there is a simple reason for it. Technology has always been invented and controlled by men, and men have always been interested in sex.

They have always been interested in money too. And photography is perhaps the best way yet devised of making money from sex. Drawings are slices of imagination: photos are slices of reality. Drawings take a long time to create: photos are created at the speed of light. Drawings depend on talent and skill: photos depend on competence. Photos are quick and convenient, easy to mass-produce and easy to conceal. They can enhance a quick one off the wrist almost anywhere and almost anytime.

The middle of the north Atlantic during one of the most vicious and one-sided sea-battles ever fought, for example. In July 1942, a convoy of thirty-five Allied merchantmen escorted by nineteen naval vessels sailed from Iceland with arms and supplies for the Soviet Union. It was a semi-suicidal voyage anyway at that time of year, when daylight is almost permanent in the far north, but *en route* news came in that the German battleship *Tirpitz* had broken through a blockade around Norway and was loose on the high seas. The naval escort was ordered to run for cover by the Admiralty and the merchantmen sailed on alone. They did not meet the *Tirpitz* (it was a false alarm), but they did meet lots of German aircraft and submarines. An American ship called The *John Witherspoon* was among the twenty-four merchantmen that never got through, and survivors from it were very lucky to be picked up by a Royal Navy corvette called *La Malouine*.

They fell asleep as soon as they lay down, at various places in the corvette, and seemed to little appreciate their great fortune. Lieutenant Caradus found one of them asleep in the officers' small bath, and ten more had taken over the wardroom and forced the wine cupboard, and were lying about the floor in a drunken stupor. The bath's tenant awoke when Caradus found him there. The Lieutenant later described: 'He had an amazing collection of nude photographs and obscene flicker photos. He pushed these cards and photos into my coat pocket. It was when I got to my cabin, after stepping over men sleeping in groups in passageways, that I saw what I had been given. Flicking the photos gave the motion-picture effect of sexual intercourse. I nearly vomited.'

The RN Lieutenant returned the man's property to him at once, and was profusely thanked for returning the crew's 'girlfriends'. The seaman said he wouldn't go anywhere without them.

This is a passage from David Irving's history of the disaster, *The Destruction of Convoy PQ.17* (Corgi, 1970), and the differing reactions of the two nationalities involved are very revealing. The British Royal Navy Lieutenant 'nearly vomited' at what the American merchant-seaman was very grateful for having returned to him. Class undoubtedly played some part too – the Lieutenant presumably being middle-class and the merchant-seaman working-class – but it is still likely to have been the case that Americans were in general more familiar with pornographic photographs than the British.

It is also likely that among the pornographic photographs owned by the American crew were some taken or printed (or both) in México. So strongly associated was early American pornography with México that the earliest and most famous examples of it were called after a Mexican border city already notorious for the easy access it afforded American citizens to prostitution and drugs:

Illustrated pamphlets depicting penetrative sex date back to the 1920s. Eight pages in length, these pamphlets – or 'Tijuana Bibles', as they came to be known – are perhaps the earliest form of comic book. Personalities of the day, whether cartoon characters (like Popeye) or gangsters (like Al Capone), were depicted in a sexually compromising position. The artist was always anonymous; so too the exact origins of the Tijuana Bibles (though it is pretty much accepted that they *didn't* come from Tijuana, more likely Los Angeles or San Diego). ['Thrill to Tales of Graphic Lust!' David Kerekes – *Critical Vision: Random Essays and Tracts Concerning Sex Religion Death*, eds David Kerekes and David Slater, Stockport, Cheshire, 1995.]

Strangely, the European equivalents of 'Tijuana Bibles' were known as 'Port Said Bibles', named from an Egyptian port with a similarly unsavoury reputation for prostitution and drugs. We see reproduced here yet another of the parallels between México and Egypt already discussed in relation to *el egipcio* Sharif Sharif. The parallel in this case is explained by the shared poverty of the two nations, and the ready supply this ensured (and still ensures) of women prepared to strip and be penetrated for the lens.

And Mexican and Egyptian women are prepared to do so despite the strong religious prohibitions placed on such behaviour in México and Egypt by, respectively, Roman Catholicism and Islam. Indeed, devout Roman Catholic women once hid the sexual allure of their hair beneath headscarves in public as devout Muslim women still do now. It seems possible, however, that religious prohibitions may have encouraged rather than discouraged the creators and manufacturers of Mexican and Egyptian pornography. The early history of porn is, for obvious reasons, difficult to trace, but it is generally agreed that in the West it began as a form of anti-clerical satire rather than as an erotic aid.

Evidence for this can be adduced from one of the underground 'classics' of literary porn to emerge from the nineteenth century. *A Man with a Maid*, written, inevitably, by an 'Anonymous' author, is the story of a man called Jack who devises an elaborate soundproofed sex-chamber for the capture and orifice-by-orifice deflowerment of a maid called Alice. Jack then goes on to maids called Fanny, Connie, Betty, and Mollie. All of whom, of course, end up enjoying it. Indeed, they all end up collaborating with it, except Betty and Mollie, who are the mother-and-daughter victims of a six-in-a-sex-chamber rape-romp that ends the book.

As you can easily infer, the book is not remarkable for its realism. You only ever feel that the author is talking about something real once, when he describes his collection of sex photos:

> Among these was a series known as the 'Crucifixion', in which a lovely girl (evidently a nun from her despoiled garments scattered on the floor) was depicted bound to a cross naked, while sometimes the Mother Abbess (in her robes), alone and sometimes in conjunction with one of the Sisters, indulged their wanton fancies and caprices on the poor girl's breasts and cunt as she hung helpless! One photograph showed the girl fastened naked to a Maltese Cross, the Lady Abbess had inserted her finger into the Nun's cunt while the Sister tickled the Nun's clitoris! In another photograph, a monk was introduced who, kneeling before the Nun (still fastened on a Maltese Cross) sucked her cunt while his uplifted hands in the attitude of prayer attacked her helpless breasts! Another series, entitled 'La Barrière', depicted various phases in the ravishment of a girl by two ruffians in a solitary part of the Bois de Boulogne. The rest were mostly scenes of Tribadism and of Lesbian love, and interspersed with them were a few representing flagellation by a girl on a girl, both being stark naked! [sic omnia]

'Interspersed' is the right word: it comes from the Latin verb *spargere*, meaning 'to scatter or sprinkle seed', which is what sex photos are really all about, is it not? We can see in the catalogue of sex photos from *A Man with a Maid*, however, that quite different motives may originally have inspired them:

the use of monks and nuns as characters in pornography is no longer especially prominent, but must have had a special political and satirical power in nineteenth-century France, a Roman Catholic country with a long history of anti-clericalism. Early Mexican pornography, it might be readily imagined, probably had similar motives, for México is also a Roman Catholic country with a long history of anti-clericalism.

Whatever its origins in satire and politics, however, pornography fulfils a single clear function today: that of masturbatory aid and, some feminists have long suggested, conditioning tool for male rapists. Other feminists have countered this argument with the claim that while masturbation in itself is no evil, pornography also serves to teach young people about things they might not otherwise easily or comfortably learn about. This is what a vulva looks like. This is what a penis looks like. This is what a vulva with a penis in it looks like. And so on. Things young people have not always learnt easily in other ways. Useful and important things, in fact.

The same sorts of things, it might be said, as have been taught by another kind of photo with a hidden history – the death photo. This is what a corpse looks like. This is what a severed head looks like. This is what a pile of human intestines looks like. And so on. Useful and important things too? Well, perhaps. But I do not think curiosity about death can explain all of some people's fascination with death photos any more than curiosity about sex can explain all of some people's fascination with sex photos. Sex remains exciting even when you know all about it. Does the same thing apply to death? For some people, I think it does. One of those people may have been the American magician and escapologist Harry Houdini (1874–1926), who saw a magician perform a cut-up body trick as a boy and:

> remained fascinated by mutilations: he possessed several grisly and much-thumbed photographs of Chinese executions, by beheading and by the death of a thousand cuts. These were images which spoke to his adult

obsessions. (*The Life & Many Deaths of Harry Houdini*, Ruth Brandon, p. 22, London, 1993)

Houdini obviously returned to those photos again and again, long after he had satisfied his curiosity about what those kinds of death looked like. Was it because he was one of the people who are excited by photos like that? Perhaps it was. But does 'excited' mean 'sexually excited'? Again, for some people, I think it does, and again, Houdini may have been one of them.

Whether or not he was, his nationality remains, I think, a significant part of the story. Houdini was an American, and the story clearly proves that, whatever his motives, he was able to obtain death photos in pre-war America. There must have been some kind of market for them just as there was for the 'Tijuana Bibles' being sold at the same time. And whatever the true origin of the Bibles, the association of Tijuana with pornography equally clearly suggests that pornography was available in México during the period. But what of death photos? Was there a market for them too in México?

This is much less easy to establish, one reason being that there are far fewer figures from Mexican culture who have received the attention figures from American culture have received, and there is consequently far less chance of relevant facts about their lives being uncovered as in the case of Harry Houdini. But there is indirect evidence that death photos would have been available in early modern México. One is that death photos are available in late modern México, to an extent, indeed, that might with only slight exaggeration be called almost ubiquitous. The fascination of contemporary Mexican newspapers and magazines with the aftermath of traffic accidents and violent crime is well known amongst *aficionados* of trash culture in the United States, but can in fact be read as the Mexican manifestation of a general characteristic of Hispanic and Roman Catholic culture.

Spain, for example, has long been more than half in love with painful death. Bullfighting, as the existence of the Graeco-Latin synonym *tauromachy* suggests, has a history stretching back for millennia, and was exported by Spain to her colonies in the New World:

### Bullfights

Each summer, four bullfights are held in Juárez at the Plaza de Toros Monumental on Av.[enida] 16 de Septiembre, beside Rio Grande Mall a bit east of Plaza de Américas. Seating up to 17,000, Monumental is the world's fourth largest bullring, and a major stop on the professional *corridas* circuit. The annual season runs April–Sept; the first *corrida de toros* takes place around Easter and then three more corridas are held on four Sundays before Labor Day. These are real Spanish-style *corridas* in which the bull may be killed by the matador. (*Northern Mexico Handbook*, Joe Cummings, Moon Publications, 1998)

The matador is an archetypal hero of Spanish-speaking culture – one book on bullfighting describes how 'a man metamorphoses into a god of the arena' (*Plaza de Toros*, Gerard & Co., Verviers, Belgium.) But his name literally means 'killer', from *matar*, 'to kill', from which is also derived *matanza*, 'slaughter, butchery, massacre'. As already described, Roman Catholicism added another ingredient to this stew of death-and-pain worship at the Renaissance, when its artists and sculptors began to represent the gory details of the Passion of Christ and the martyrdom of his saints with a hyper-realism designed to cement the allegiance of the faithful and encourage their attendance at church. One common image of Roman Catholic iconography remains, for example, the *corazón sagrada*, the sacred heart, in which Christ folds open the flesh of his left breast to reveal his blood-dripping, thorn-pierced heart.

The exportation of such images to México found a fertile soil for naturalisation and continued growth, for the native traditions of México contained similar obsessions, which hybridised with Spanish imports to produce such uniquely Mexican psycho-cultural artefacts as *el Día de los Muertos*: the Day of the Dead:

México's third most important festival . . . Some of the festivities are held in cemeteries where families clean the headstones and crucifixes of their deceased relatives (*los defuntos*), decorate them with flowers, and play games unique to this fiesta. In some areas the faithful will spend a whole day and night beside the family graves in a cemetery. Even roadside shrines throughout México are laid with fresh flowers and other tributes to the dead. Offerings of *pan de los muertos* ('bread of the dead') and food and liquor are placed before family altars, along with papier-mâché skulls and skeletons. (*Northern Mexico Handbook*, Joe Cummings, Moon Publications, 1998)

Such festivals have nourished a Hispano-Mexican obsession with death and its liquid concomitants that expanded eagerly to occupy the new media of photography, film, and television. One can readily see such things as the following on Mexican television – and at breakfast-time:

The camera pans a suicide. The man is quite young and wearing a bulky blue sweater. By his feet is a five-gallon bucket. The rope around his neck is tied to a small tree in a city park. His neck is bent but the rope is straight and taut. The camera frames the man and the tree, then zooms in to peruse his body, and quickly does a 180-degree pan around to his neck. The camera zooms in again to one of his feet. It is touching the ground during the hours he spent hanging here alone, the man's neck stretched and now he is firmly planted on the earth again. ('While You Were Sleeping', Charles Bowden)

Such scenes run 'every morning at 7:45 a.m.' on a television station in Juárez as 'a special eight- to ten-minute part of the morning news', and must reflect something about the tastes and propensities of Juárez's inhabitants. Undoubtedly, some viewers must enjoy watching scenes like that, just as they must enjoy newspaper pictures of crash victims and gang murders. But can one pass moral judgments on such pleasures, and extrapolate from them to behaviour? Could, for example, the saturation of the Mexican media by images of death and pain have contributed something to the Juárez serial murders? In short, is there something wrong – and dangerous – about someone who enjoys and is attracted to such images?

For me, the answer is yes. There is something wrong with someone like that. Wrong, but interesting too. That people should enjoy looking at sex photos is not really interesting: it is what you would expect. That people should enjoy looking at death photos is not what you would expect. That people should be sexually excited by death photos – as some undoubtedly are – is even less what you would expect. The question raised by it must be: Why?

And the answer must be something to do with maleness. Like technology, culture is created and driven by men, and most areas of culture are dominated by men too. Death photos are part of what you might call splatter-culture, and splatter-culture is created, driven, and dominated by men. It is men who make horror videos, sell them, and watch them, and it is men who trade in and collect death photos. Just as it is men who trade in and collect postage stamps, telephone cards, and child pornography. There are general male characteristics of obsession and acquisitiveness at work in each hobby, but for death photos and child porn I think there are some more particular male characteristics at work too. One of them is, I would say, a greater tendency to perversion, which is based on a greater tendency to neurological abnormality.

As I said previously, there is something wrong with people who enjoy looking at death photos, and whatever is wrong with them must be present in their brains. Male brains are much likelier to be *abnormal* than female brains. Jack the Ripper's brain was abnormal, for example, but then so was Albert Einstein's, it is just that Jack the Ripper's abnormal brain probably owed at least as much to male environment as to male genes. The male environment has always been more violent than the female one, and males get attacked and injured more often. This is true in all cultures, which differ merely in attack and murder rates while always maintaining a higher and lower rate of, respectively, male and female victimisation. The murder rate in México is one of the highest in the world, for example, but only for men.